SEX FOR SUCCESS

Chennai • Bangalore

CLEVER FOX PUBLISHING

Chennai, India

Published by CLEVER FOX PUBLISHING 2023

Copyright © Girish Kumar Kashwani 2023

All Rights Reserved.

ISBN: 978-93-60764-67-8

This book has been published with all reasonable efforts to ensure the material is error-free with the author's consent. No part of this book shall be used or reproduced in any manner whatsoever without written permission from the author. Girish Kumar Kashwani asserts the moral right to be identified as the author of this work. This book offers educational information and is not a substitute for financial, business, or career advice. Seek guidance from a subject matter expert. The book perfectly supplements the author's real-world boot camp program, a viable option for those who do not want to pursue a full-time MBA degree program.

The Publisher does not endorse or guarantee the reliability, accuracy, or completeness of the Content in this book. The Publisher and author shall not be liable for any errors, omissions, or claims for loss or damages arising out of the use of the information contained in this book.

Cover: **Girish Kumar Kashwani**

YOU ARE LOVE.

Come. Sit. Watch

Dedicated to you

May you become the extraordinary
millennial of the 21st century,
the legendary, a complete man,
a complete woman,
"rich outside, richer inside."

That is my intention for you and the world.

My Gratitude

My Mother, for the sacrifices she made for us to live a life of abundance. My Daughter, the love of my life for eternity. My Son, for teaching me that being a good human being can be a goal, too. Shri N.S. Srivatsa is the man who inspired and helped me become an entrepreneur. Shri S.S.P Khurana, the man who is like a Godfather, is always with me for me unconditionally.

In loving memories of
my beloved mother, the late
Smt. Kaushalya Kashwani.

Girish kashwani

CONTENTS

SEX IS THE SECRET	9
SEX MADE SIMPLE	11
MIND DESTROYS HEART CREATES	18
WHY SEX FOR SUCCESS	25
THE IDEA CALLED SUCCESS	28
EDUCATION OF MIND IS THE EDUCATION OF SLAVERY	30
RICH BEGGAR, POOR BEGGAR	34
HOW TO USE SEX FOR SUCCESS THE THEHNIQUE	39
ALL THINGS BEAUTIFUL BELONG TO THE HEART	42
MIND AND MONEY MATTERS	44
LOVE AND LET LOVE DO	46
TRANSFORM INSIDE OUT	49
FROM HOPELESSNESS TO HOPE	51
IT IS THE QUESTION OF YOUR LIFE	52
SPECIFIC IS TERRIFIC	56
YOU ARE A BORN LEGEND	57
BEST IS NOT A COMPETITION, IT IS A QUALITY	60
EXPERIENCE IS THE ONLY WAY IN AND OUT	63
ENTREPRENEURSHIP IS A MINDSET MADE OF HEART	68

THE BEGINNING	71
CHARACTER MATTERS	73
THE ONLY COURAGE IS TO BE WHAT YOU WANT TO BE	77
OUT OF CHAOS, A NEW MAN IS BORN	85
TRUST IS THE ONLY DEGREE WORTHY OF EDUCATION	98
IN THE KINGDOM OF GOD, ZERO IS A HERO	104
LIVE SESSIONS	119
LIVE SESSIONS ADVANCE LEVEL	143
EVERY BEGINNING HAS AN END	160
DO-IT-YOURSELF TECHNIQUES	161
PROJECT WORKS	165
CLOSING PRAYERS	167
AUTHOR'S COORDINATES	170

Sex Is The Secret

For centuries, the debate has been on how the first men and women were born. I am neither a saint nor a scientist, nor do I want to be one; I am simply happy being me! So, to me, the only way humans, and of course even animals, can be born is when a male and a female have intercourse, which is called sex, but to me, intercourse is just one of the arms of a wheel called sex. In rare cases, just one intercourse, a miracle happens! In some cases, after many, and in a few cases, all efforts fail; one hopes for a miracle! I believe this gives birth to the most complicated question of humankind: why me? And this also would have been the first time human beings would have invented the word "The Problem"! on which we all men and women for over centuries are surviving and thriving, "solving problems," in the name of kings, queens, politicians' husbands, wife, children, businessmen, business women, workers, every man, and woman on this planet in some way or the other is busy solving problem for a better tomorrow! Do you ever wonder what would happen if the word problem did not exist? What you and I must have been doing! Be careful; I am watching your thoughts! So, agree or not, sex is the origin of the problem, whether a miracle happens or not! Sex is the reason we strive to work and work harder than ever before because that better tomorrow has not yet come! And problems to be solved have multiplied and have become more complicated! And every solution by the man and woman that promises to make tomorrow a better day to live! The promise of success has created another problem: failure; remember the famous quote, "Success and failure are two sides of one coin," fits so well here! So next time when you feel you are successful, be alert! And when you think of the other as a failure, be more attentive! Who knows who will win the toss tomorrow?

So, to me, sex also, in a way, is the origin of what human beings have defined as their success and failure. As long as humanity exists, sex will remain the mother of all inventions because, with every problem, with every failure, there arises the hope that a miracle will happen one day, that someone will succeed, and that a better tomorrow will come.

Desire is the seed.

Existence. Sex. Life

Sex Made Simple

We are living in the 21st century, the so-called Sex, the male and the female, and having physical intimacy is far simpler than ever before. Most developed societies have opened the doors for sex talks, sex education, and sexual experience as much as having multiple partner experiences before committing to one for a lifetime problem! I mean the marriage. Once upon a time, a boy and a girl met before marriage to set expectations about money, work, relationships, and family values to settle for life. Now, a boy and a girl meet to set sexual expectations! and the beauty is that Sex is the only expectation in the history of humankind that has no limits; no one can set the rules for life! It is gender-neutral; instead, men are under more pressure to perform! Available in abundance as much as the existence, free! Until the last breath and beyond! And the best part is, Sex is the only expectation on earth that changes with the moment and the mood! So, at any point, the expectation can fail; it all depends on the mood. Whose! Remember the famous saying, "Behind every successful man, there is a woman." Got it!

So, we must remember Sex not only gives birth to bodies but Sex also gives birth to the qualities called "feeling" and "desire." The "desire" for a better experience makes men and women do more! Innovate more! Ye Dil Mange more! Be it Sex, money, or happiness.

So here I bring you the events that caused the eternal miracle! I heard God was bored one day; he wanted to have fun! And out of that desire, he created man and woman to have fun! Who is the first? Only God knows! So, with all sincerity, I can say the story of the desire of God is just like that old Hindi movie, where the male and female are in love, alone in a dense forest, drenched in the rain, stuck in a thunderstorm, in a cage, looking at each other in such a way as if their eyes are for doing Sex! Suddenly, a garden with flowers of every possible color and type kissing each other appears for you to imagine what is happening inside! So, if the story is true, those two would have been the last man and woman on earth because only God can produce just by desiring! The rest of us must have Sex to make miracles! So, to put it simply, to me, through Sex, God created what is said to be the most beautiful, the miraculous invention of God, the men and the women, and it seems God has been having unlimited fun.

So, remember, the invention of Sex is the supreme invention, and that's why God remains the foremost inventor because who invented Sex? It is God, the unknown, an existential quality, a birthright. Therefore, to me, Sex and God are synonymous, and that is why it is true to say Sex is God. Beauty is every living being in the universe: the men, the women, the birds, the animals, the flowers; everyone has it and experiences it, and that is why, while every minutest particle in existence is different and unique, Sex is the only commonality, and if not for God but for the Sex, we are all one, "All in one, one in all." Sex is our original identity, the male and female Sex! I do not know about animals, but as the man and the woman grow, everything in their life changes but one, the desire, the only constant, until the last breath, and after that, God knows!

I have yet to come across a man or a woman who does not aspire to become the CEO of their unicorn or as a working professional rising on to the dream position, the ultimate real-world success for which twenty-two years or more of precious lifetime we invest in going to school and colleges and the outcome, here are some fact checks for you;

Did You Know

- 80% of engineering graduates in India are unemployable
- 55% of MBA graduates are unemployable
- 64% of teachers say they want to provide holistic education to youths but lack time and resources
- 74% of employers say youths are not ready to face the Real-world challenges at workplaces lack social and emotional skills
- 80% of Startups fail within one year, and only 10% survive beyond five years
- 70% of youths graduate with degrees having no specific industry needs
- Only one in twelve entrepreneurs succeed in building successful businesses
- Only 1% of professionals make it to the dream CXO run
- As per the Human Development Report, India ranks 132 in the Human Development Index amongst 191 countries (2021-2022).

So, have you heard the one-liner in every religion? The great masters have said repeatedly, "Tatvamasi- "you are that," you carry within you the potential to become the God, just you have been made to forget your true potential! If you are with me, you must be able to feel the godly power within you, the energy of sex, that if you can recall again in some way if you become aware of it, you can become the father and mother of all CEOs ever born on the earth, The God! The Supreme CEO. Be either extraordinary or nothing.

Sex is the mother of an eternal invention called experience.

Desire. Sex. Experience. God

Here, can you see the fallacy of societies and the education system? If you would not feel like going to school and college because you may be intelligent! The family and society will term you as abnormal, and we are all social animals, and animals do not have minds of their own! By this logic, in no way am I saying that all children and youths should stop going to schools and colleges or the educational institutions must close; that would be like being part of the problem, and as such, so many families are dependent on educational institutions that I would say schools and colleges are now running less for their core purpose of imparting proper knowledge and developing global professionals and human beings, instead running so that the wheel of the economy keeps moving, economy the fulcrum of building a prosperous society, the societies of we the social animals! Money matters!

So, I repeat, school and colleges must go on! And you also go on! The real challenge for youth is, in the process of fulfilling socio-economic obligations, for the social animals to remain in control and routine; they are required to succeed in a race in which no one knows where they are running, what they are running for, how long the race is going to be, no one knows on which field, which track the race is! The only teaching they have is to keep running and be focused! And on track! And to be an excellent social animal!

The irony is that in the name of preparation to succeed in the race of life, examinations have become the lifeline where marks decide your success and failure. As I shared above, this racing mechanism is an utter failure and will continue because life is so vibrant, dynamic, and ever-changing from moment to moment. What does it know about our marks or which language we speak? Life knows no language; life knows no failures. If there was a possibility to give life another name, it must be a success; life is a success, you being born as a human being is a tremendous success, you are the greatest success, you are life, you are God, you need to drop out of the race of full filling the obligations, the expectations and you are a winner, here and now! Simply because life is here and now in this moment. So be there in society, school, and college. Where else to go? Nowadays, the best place to open schools and colleges and build homes is the forests, so wherever you go, the school and colleges and we, the animals, follow you. So be there, run your race, find your field, and be on your track.

Know that success and life are waiting for you. A great master has said that with every child born, life still has hopes that someone will sing her songs, dance her way, and make millions celebrate life! One in billions, in centuries, succeeds; a miracle happens! And life is happy and prosperous. I wish you may become that one in a billion, sing the song of success, dance your way to success, become eternally triumphant, become one with life, and be always full of life.

Whenever you see a child born, remember life has succeeded.

Sing. Dance. Celebrate. Rejoice

Mind Destroys Heart Creates

Just in the past 100 years, humanity has suffered five wars: World War I, World War II, the Korean War, the Vietnam War, the Cold War, and the Gulf War; millions have died, and millions are dying while I am writing, and millions of innocent children becoming orphaned, and homeless. Can you feel the suffering of a man or a woman who goes through destruction when war happens if left alive by God's grace? And here, if you think, you can feel, let me tell you, it is superficial, just like hearing the news of someone close passing away, you worry, you feel sad for a few days, and you move on; what else can you do otherwise, you must live! And here is one of the greatest secrets I am giving you: the only way to experience the feeling of the other is when one has become love, and love knows no different; in the moment of true love, two become one, and when you have experienced that oneness there is no way one can kill oneself! Treat this as my diamond sutra; this is the real meaning of "Empathy," a quality that societies and educational institutions worldwide expect youths to develop to become successful in creating a loving, peaceful, and harmonious society for us, the social animals! Tomorrow. I call this education a humiliation to God and societies as hypocrites, misleading our children! The ask is correct, but the way of doing it is disastrous.

You must have heard success lies in execution, and the essential criterion of becoming empathetic is being in love with oneself! For simple understanding, consider Empathy as a family member of love, and the way to love is through our hearts. Can you see the beauty of love here and why, in every religion, all masters have said "God is love "? Thou shalt love thy neighbors as thyself. "Vasudhaiva kutumbakam one earth, one family." Therefore, you can see that our education, the education of mind, is producing us the killers, the societies of killers! And remember, killing does not mean only by guns and bombs and missiles; just make a child, a youth, feel like a failure, and you have killed a life! So why that a better tomorrow is never a possibility? Because we, the killers of today, are teaching the youths to kill today but expecting them to be loving tomorrow. Training mind, hoping they develop heart, I call it the ultimate calamity, the chaos. Centers of knowledge, peace, prosperity, and life have become turmoil centers. We have forgotten even the basics of our lord Buddha's teaching, who said, be the change you want to see! Does it not shake us for a second what we are going to schools and colleges for? In the quest to become CEOs, we are becoming CKOs, the chief killing officers.

The educated mind is the most powerful weapon in the world.

Sw. Viveka Nanda

"A real education will not
teach you to compete;
it will lead you to cooperate.

It will not teach you to fight and
come first; it will teach
you to be creative, loving,
and blissful, without any
comparison with others".

OSHO

So, you can see the calamity that is happening; institutions must teach Love to develop prosperous, peaceful, and harmonious human beings, which is the core purpose of education, and the beauty is it needs no degrees, no certificates. Can you ever imagine someone carrying a certificate, Ph.D., in Love? And the miracle is, Love is available free, twenty-four hours a day! Not in schools, colleges, or even your homes; it is in your heart. And remember," home is where the heart is. "Do not forget that not only humans, the animals, the trees, the rivers, the mountains, the sky, the air, the sun, the moon, the stars, and every minute particle in existence is vibrating with Love. But we have forgotten that the heart is the door to love, God, and life. We are searching, asking for God, door to door! Because where is the education that teaches me and you the qualities of the heart, teaches us about our very own nature, Love? Our textbooks have no mention of those masters in whose names we go to temples, churches, or mosques; Love is their only message. Love has disappeared from textbooks; destruction is the only guarantee of the outcome.

So, our education is like you and me doing a headstand! The famous sheers asana. We are standing upside down! Instead of teaching the way of love and peace, it is teaching cutthroat competition and aggression to kill. Education is simply fooling us in the name of teaching us success, making us an utter failure because that better tomorrow has never come; it has been centuries.

I wish through this book that you stand up straight and dance your way to heart, to the kingdom of God, and become eternally loving and successful human beings; Love is the only success.

So, you, the 21st-century youths, have far more freedom to experience sex compared to our generation and a few generations before ours until the time the famous Khajuraho temple became a vulgar spot! I am writing this book for the youth, professionals, and entrepreneurs of the 21st century, ready to become extraordinary millennials and complete professionals, "rich outside, richer inside."

My effort through this book is to rekindle that sleeping power within you by imparting those secret codes of success that have transformed an ordinary man and a woman into legendary professionals and human beings for centuries.

Such is the power you carry within you to be what you want to be. Let me remind you that becoming God, the supreme CEO, is your possibility, and this life is your opportunity. Look at the irony; we, the born emperors, have become living beggars just that some of us are rich beggars, and some are poor beggars.Education has failed us miserably.

May this book help you, guide you, and connect you with that supreme power, which is yours, within you, and may you become the extraordinary, the masterpiece you are born to write your own story.

Educating the mind without educating the heart is no education at all.

Aristotle

Why Sex For Success

By now, if you have been with me or even otherwise, whoever believes in God! would agree that God is the most powerful, the supreme of us all, but here, I would say it is either Sex or God. I choose Sex as supreme because I do not know anything about God, do not even know whether God is a male or a female, just heard of God; even to say heard is wrong because, whenever there is a situation in which I can't handle and ranges from having an upset stomach to not getting a job, business not doing well or when I feel no one is listening to me, no one is loving me, during those times, I think of God! Other than that, just an idea! As I see it, this is the root cause for humanity touching the lowest levels because we are using someone called God for our benefit to help us, not even knowing whether it is he or she who at least sees whether we need the help of female or male God! and that is why you see, millions of us praying to God to take us out of sufferings of wars, of struggles, of chaos. Still, it seems God is not listening at all! And we eventually drop the idea of God! Without realizing this foolish mistake, we are not specific, and we, the billions, are always calling God simultaneously to the supreme CEO to listen! The outcome is perfect; the CEO has instructed the secretary to reject the noise and maintain silence! And the worst part is even dogs we know their Sex, but God never even thought of enquiring to study who God is, our supreme CEO, to whom we all must report in person; time is the only factor, at least to get introduced, so when the time comes, we are not caught unaware! So, we have an idea of God! but what about Sex? We know, we see, we feel, we identify, we experience, and we are born out of Sex, the power through which even God is born!

The Rama, The Krishna, The Buddha, The Kabeer, The Nanak, The Meera, The Mahaveera. I am purposefully not writing, The God Jesus! I love him so much because there are sayings that Jesus was born from the Virgin Mother Mary, and I have no intention of creating a controversy. I am not an enlightened spiritual master; I am just an ordinary man and happy being me. I am a Hindu, and in our scriptures, all our Gods and Goddesses are born through their parents! Just like you and me, the beauty is almost all of them were princes and princesses, and nearly all went through the deepest of hardships and chaos in their lifetimes; some chose, some forced, and out of the chaos, a new man and a new woman, the Gods, and the Goddesses were born. So that is why, to me, Sex is the supreme power because Sex is the only way to become a man or a woman and experience Godliness, become God, the supreme of all.

Now, before you judge my book by its cover, let me tell you, my book is not about how to use Sex to become the God, the enlightened one, though by the title, you must have felt mine is a cheap gimmick using Sex to sell! Think otherwise! Sex does sell! It is Sex only that sells! The more you are with me, the more you will not only experience but you will master the art of using Sex for success to become legendary. Thinking crazy, me, I am loving it!

So, my intention is not to get into details of our education system, how we can revive it, in which century Kamasutra was part of the Indian education system, which the teachers were, what the syllabus was, and the process! Neither am I going to advocate that the current education system must include Sex in the syllabus. It is best left for policymakers to decide, and as such, I do not see much changing with education and societies; the roots of evils have gone too deep; all the social ills what we call competition, anger, 21st-century fomo, anxiety, comparison, failures, depression, mental pressure, etc. enters a child's life the day one they put their first step in the school. Imagine if there were no schools. Would any of us know the meaning of success and failure? A food for thought!

So rather than developing global human beings, which is the urgent need for a better today! We are busy building more and more schools and colleges for a better tomorrow! That is why I initially said I have no intention of becoming part of a problem. Instead, I have a solution, and that is precisely what my book is to introduce you to that knowledge that does not interfere with your regular education and develops you as a global professional and a human being in a fraction of time and cost. It gives you the power to choose; it gives you the power to be what you want to be. How! Come. Sit. Watch, the journey has just begun, a trip that starts with you and ends with YOU. You transform! You become a new man, a new woman, the original, the masterpiece. Such is your glory, you are that, "Tatvamasi.'

**Mind is for science,
heart for art, poetry, music,
and the transcendental
for religion.
Unless an education serves
all these things, it is not true.**

OSHO

The Idea Called Success

So, if you have been with me, you would agree that sex is the key to heavenly success! And before you think any further, whether to agree with me or not, I request you take a pause here and think, in your twenty-two years of education, every moment, at the core, you have been taught success, but has anyone taught you, what is the meaning of success, where does success live, what is its age, what is your relationship with success, is success a male or female sex! How much is good to have! For a moment, you may think, what a crazy question, but think otherwise! For one Idea called success that I and you live and die every moment of our precious life, running behind, cutting throats, we have no idea about! You are on a blind date! The accident is inevitable! If you can escape, you succeed! So, be more careful before running behind the success, the mystery girl, or the mysterious boy! What you say! So here is the secret to success: know sex, know success. No sex, no success.! just for fun.

Now, the questions you might have: how to unlock the door of heaven! Who would want to miss heaven? It's a matter of courage! Just that you do not know where the teacher is to push! Which university, India or overseas? Online or offline! And here you need to think otherwise because my book is not to teach you about which sexual posture will give you or your partner the ultimate pleasure, the ultimate success!

You might know this better than me or read Kamasutra! You must have read already! I have told you physical intercourse, which is known as sex, is just one arm of the wheel; otherwise, every human being on earth would have become legendary either reading Kamasutra or watching online free, available all-time, everywhere, where ever you go, you need to find your time and space, and you succeed!

No, the real power of sex is beyond physical intimacy, beyond intercourse. But for you to know the power of the wheel called sex, it is too late, not because you are not ready, but because the whole of education, our upbringing, our minds have been developed to suppress, to kill that knowledge through which you can know the power of wheel, the sex. The power to become the supreme, the emperor, the supreme is suppressed. The whole education system has enslaved us, and that is what Britishers wanted. We, the enslaved people, and you very well know our entire education is the design of the famous lord Macaulay, whose famous speech in the British parliament still gets a frequent reference on social media, which says the only way to enslave the Indians was to cut the roots of their education. Macauley is smiling, watching us from heaven!

Education Of Mind Is The Education Of Slavery

So far, if you have any doubts, let that be well settled here: while we are physically independent, our minds are still the minds of an enslaved person, and with every passing day, we are making the roots of slavery more vital because our education is still the education of slavery, the education of Macaulay. We all know that the mind does what it is programmed to do. Slavery is programmed day in and day out, and our mind is doing its it's jobs perfectly; that is why we are the best laborers in the world and some of our western emperors, who give us jobs, call us even computer coolies, because we are best in doing! Software coding, I mean! And the icing on the cake is, always available from morning till evening, to do best!

So, with this kind of slave mindset, if I teach you about the other arms of the wheel called Sex, which are compassion, empathy, caring, and kindness, it will be impossible to understand because for over centuries and generations, our education has only taught us that success lies in money, power, and in material pleasures, which is possible to achieve by making the mind more robust, the more the mind is strong more one can go for the kill! Who! Note, the mind and reason do not know relationships; whoever comes their way of power, money, and pleasure! Men, women, nature, anything, kill to achieve, cut-throat; the more one cuts, the more successful. But compassion, caring, empathy, and kindness are all the qualities of the heart, the fulcrum on which the wheel of Sex rotates; remember a very significant difference here: the heart is our eternal companion; we are born with it; ask a mother about the first heartbeat of her child and watch the thrill, the wonders in her eyes, love is miraculous! But we all know the mind develops while growing up, copying up! And to know heart and love, we need to drop our minds! Mind and heart do not meet. They can never meet; they do not even know they are neighbours! Such is the education, a mess, a chaos. Remember the famous saying, "Men are from Mars, women are from Venus." Did you get it? Keep it food for thought.

So, to understand heart or love, we need to go within, without mind! Because our minds are programmed to go outside, to run, for name, fame, money, power, position, luxuries, and Sex, all are out; nobody has taught us how to go inside! Because it is not part of the syllabus, where is the time for love? Finding time for Sex itself is so difficult! So let me tell you the education of going within without the mind is called "meditation," of which lord Macauley cut the roots because Meditation is the education of the "heart, "whose language is "silence, "and the outcome is, finding your authentic power, finding the original you, which is love. And this is what Jesus has said so simply: God is love, and a great Indian master has said love is GOD. You do not know God, no worries, know love, know God, and realize you are God. Love is the power, the treasure; you have it, I have it, everyone has it. Knowledge and education make all the difference. And this is the meaning when one says knowledge is power! I add that proper knowledge is the power through which one realizes we are all love; we are all one, connected, one in all, all in One. Love is the power, the supreme creator, the energy of the universe, Tatvamasi- You are that.

The word meditation may be familiar to you. You might have even tried going to a spiritual master or yoga classes in your way, which is part of the meditation process.

So, in one way or another, millions and millions have been trying to meditate, do yoga and pranayama, do prayers, go to church, go to mosques, go to the temple. Whoever does, the purpose must be to become peaceful, loving, happy, healthy, wealthy, and to live a long life, to do what! Ask this question from an older man or woman in the nursing home, the parents of a successful man and woman! Not theirs, but your heart will cry!

So, the outcome of the doing! There are more wars, more killings, more mental and psychological diseases, loneliness, despair, and depression. So basically, while millions of us are praying and doing for heaven! It seems doctors, hospitals, and psychologists are having good times!

What is happening? There seems to be something fundamentally wrong with so many yoga teachers, spiritual masters, great doctors, and scientists and having every possible material comfort on earth; the world would have been a heaven to live in today, and now you know why we are studying and working so hard for that better tomorrow. Any guesses? So, what if it is hell today? Tomorrow, heaven will fall on earth! We will succeed.

Now, where I am coming from is that if I start telling you about love with this state of mind, it will be a mere time pass; you may enjoy it because that is our common core, our fulcrum, universal fulcrum every cell of our body is vibrating with love, you must have heard, love is universal! so just the remembrance is a joy. Still, we do not feel it; we have become stone-like, living stones, and we do not even know that we have become that! Can you understand this? We have no idea that if it is not love, we will die; a matter of time! Love is the life force, the life energy, and we have no idea of life, of love! And this ignorance is because we are programmed to live in mind! And to regain our real nature, the love, we must become uneducated! And here comes the most famous quote of the 21st century you must have heard: Learn. Unlearn. Relearn.," more used by IT companies to motivate their employees to keep them on their toes! Now you can see why the engineering degree has become the "queen" of all the degrees and the dream of every graduate of India to become an IT engineer! IT professionals are the chosen ones to find solutions for a better tomorrow! It is a lifetime Job, settled for a lifetime!

**Love is the fulcrum
sex is the wheel.**

Love. Meditation. Silence. YOU

Rich Beggar Poor Beggar

I am sure now you have some idea about love, you know where love resides, you know how to find love, and let me tell you, if you have understood even this much, trust me, you are one in millions! But the mind will ask what to do now, what is the use! Just ignore mind for now! Let this reality sink in; you are unique and chosen, and you will know how love works without working and without making noise, silently the secret of all secrets.

Whether you know or not, you accept it or not, subconsciously, all our doing from birth to death is for love, to get love, and sex is the closest experience of love, and that is why the desire remains till the last breath and the wheel goes on. Are you with me? The irony is that we are all trying to get love by doing something or from anybody, and nobody seems to satisfy! And this is the disaster, and here is top secret revealing: all kinds of doing is of mind, whole education is of the reason, of doing and becoming, which means you do and you get! You take an exam, and you get marks. You get good marks, parents get you, apple! I mean mobile. So, if one asks me what the outcome of twenty-two years of education is, my answer is that we learn how to become the best beggars; the sugar-coated word is "expectation. "We understand what and how to expect from others. Are you with me? And the peak of human foolishness is when we, the educated beggars, go to spiritual masters, asking how to be happy, peaceful, and loving! I can tell you with all authenticity one atom bomb of blessing they will drop on you! They will ask you to drop expectations! Poor man, it is an eternal truth! Women, it seems they live more in heart! But as I see, there is no difference anymore because we are living in the age of gender neutrality, so I say the poor men and the poor women!

Through this book, I wish you, the 21st century men and women, to become one in love again. May you experience that pure love in which the expectations drop, the mind drops, and the other disappears! May you become that love that knows no others! May you become the new men and the new women "Rich Outside, Richer Inside." Asking how! We are getting closer! Please take a deep breath, and let's move deeper!

So, I hope it is clear to you that all doing is of mind, and all dependency is of sense, even for love! And that is why the so-called sex has become such a mess because sex also has become a doing, just like a job, faster the better! It is the 21st century, speed matters, you see! and everyone thinks sex is love! So, the more you try to be loving, or the more you try to be peaceful, the more you become angry and restless because your mind is trying to achieve what does not belong to it! But unfortunately, the only knowledge we have is how to expect! Nobody has taught us how not to expect! So, the mind has no clue. It has become a wanderer, and the symptoms of this situation are anger, frustration, and depression; name any mental disease, the root lies in expectation, and from where the root developed, education! The irony is because of this education, millions of doctors, spiritual masters, motivational speakers, hospitals, and shopping centres are doing great business and giving employment to thousands of people, so if the miracle happens, education changes to heart, and that tomorrow comes today! What will happen to the economy, to the society? Are you with me? Can you understand this?

The other name for this situation of man is called the madman. And slowly, we either drop out or lose faith in love and god, the ultimate failure, the last failure, and this is the harm the education has done; it has destroyed the power within you to the extent that you do not even know you are born emperor, love is the essence of your being, you cannot lose it, it is your nature, you are born out of love, alas, we the educationist, the teachers, the parents, whom you trusted upon, we have misled you, we have taken away your real nature from you, which you are searching for, looking for asking for! And we certainly can't give you, because we do not have it. Remember, one can only give what one has! So, your authentic power, the power of enquiring and questioning, is suppressed because if you ask who you are, who will answer? Schools and colleges have to appoint Love gurus! It is an illegal act. And even if they do! Who has a Ph.D. in love? Still, I say to you, be courageous, ask again! and I promise you, your heart is waiting to answer; change the quality of questioning, do not ask from anybody this time, forgive us all for our ditches and for the first time sit and ask the rising sun, the moon, the stars, the early morning breeze, the sea, ask and ask sincerely, honestly, with total trust. I guarantee you will find each one waiting for you for eternity to answer! In that trust, you become one with existence because another name of existence is trust; you will become love because another name of existence is love, always giving, always waiting; someday, someone will ask, who are you? And your real nature, the secret of all secrets, will be revealed by the god or call it existence, love, or life. Can you see the miracle? It is 21st century, specific is terrific!

That is why I initially said I am not a spiritual master, and I neither want to become one; I am happy being me! So, my way of telling you the secret code of success, which of course is love, is your way, a way that you can relate to, and once you can connect, you will easily be able to find your way to experience, and that is where the secret of success lies, you experiencing the power of love, yourself and what becomes your experience, you become that, you become love, you become successful, that one in billions, the legendary, this is my intention for you and the world.

**Existence is your
real companion.**

Listen. Calling. Waiting

Having come together so far, I feel now is the time to introduce you to the power of love, the fulcrum on which the wheel of sex is moving; we, the men and women, are moving! I am purposely saying introduction because, as I said, with the current mindset, only the basics can be understood by you. After all, it has nothing to do with the mind, but we all know we are all full of mind, the mindful! And except for the word heart, which beats somewhere inside our body and its shape, which has become the symbol of love, absolutely nothing else we know about our own heart.

HOW TO USE SEX FOR SUCCESS

THE TECHNIQUE

The technique is effortless: being with your own heart more! Currently, your entire upbringing and education have developed you as a strong mind because the current educators have said to you that to succeed in the world, which simply means to have more money and more power, you need a strong mind, and they are right; only the strong mind can kill, the stronger, the more killings, more wars, more power! A soft mind means a strong heart! The heart knows only love. Love is the essence of creation; therefore, love is the superpower in the real sense. Now, you may be unable to feel or see whether you are in the mind or the heart! And it is perfectly alright, and let me tell you, if you are feeling confused now, know that you have the first secret key to open the golden door, the door to heart! Confusion is good sometimes!

The immediate thought could be how to be more with heart and how it leads to success. By now, you know that education, which is the education of the mind, has failed utterly and continuously. If you can see correctly, failure begins with the day the child goes to school; otherwise, the child is perfect, born successful until compared with the others. The calamity is that all the education given to a child is for success, and the most significant harm the education is doing is not teaching the child that behind every successful child, there is failure! So now here you have another secret key; the heart knows no other! And when there is no other, you are original, innocent, happy, fun-loving, playful, child-like. And one fine day, you were expelled from your home, from heaven to a school! Thrown out from the garden of Eden, what was your sin? Which apple did you eat? Who was the snake that told you to eat? Any guesses? Let me say that we, the men and women, are the snakes; success is the apple; we made you eat! And remember, this is not philosophy; as we move together, you will realize, with this simple understanding, you have found the greatest treasure of your life, yourself, the original, you, the creator, the masterpiece! A skill for which youths are paying millions, how to become creative thinkers! to create a better tomorrow! Are you laughing? Laugh more! Let Macauley feel jealous for a change!

Love knows no other.

All in one. One in all

All Things Beautiful Belong To The Heart

You must have heard that all that is beautiful in the universe reflects the quality of a heart! Have you also heard that all creativity is of heart? I say destruction is of mind, and this is the calamity. A child, the most beautiful creation of existence, of nature, having the potential to realize their existential nature, gets educated and becomes the destroyer of their creator, their nature!

To me, it is not the atomic bomb that is the most dangerous creation of humankind; it is the education system that is the most dangerous creation, which develops a beautiful, innocent child into a man who goes on to make an atomic bomb to kill their people. The height of foolishness of we human beings is while the nuclear bomb was made once, for over centuries, every moment a child is being sent to school getting the same education, hoping for a happy, loving, and peaceful tomorrow! and obviously, it never comes, it cannot!

So, having introduced to the power of love, whose home is our own heart, you must want to know what is my technique of teaching by which you will realize the energy of love yourself, without philosophical lectures, without being a spiritual master and degree, called enlightenment, signed by God! And how that will make you a legendary professional, "rich outside, richer Inside." So, let us explore and learn the techniques.

Education is not the amount of information put into your brain and runs riots there, undigested, all your life.

Sw. Vivekananda

Mind And Money Matters

So now you might have got some conviction that it is essential to be with the heart. But the real question at this point in your mind might be that money, position, and power are necessary for living, and all of this needs a brain, so the mind is your best friend, and the heart is a pure time pass! In that way, school and colleges are your real homes because you earn money after education and can survive, at least! What will you get being with heart, with love? Who will give a job being in love? What business of love and passion can you think of?

Here, you may find my answer crazy, but I say to you, while your question is correct, this very thinking is the root cause of all the evils of humanity. Education has rejected the heart, left the love, and in doing this, education has denied all that is beautiful: the sun, the moon, the stars, and the existence that has never failed! Existence knows no failure, which means heart knows no failure, which only means love is the only success, just if one can guide you; I am purposefully not using word teaching because a teacher in the original form of education was just a guide, not a teacher but a master! You will know more about the way of authentic education and its beauty. For now, you need to know how to be friends with your own heart, and you are ready to explore the most thrilling adventure of your life, the mother of all adventures; you are on a journey to be friends with YOU, and remember YOU are wealthy of all riches.

You are a treasure; you must know how to unlock it and see for yourself! You are the prince and the princess, the kings and the queens. Alas, we, the emperors, are happy being beggars! Why? What is wrong? Macaulay, education is the problem. Satisfied! or Dill Mange More!

So now it brings me to the point of showing you how to develop a friendship with heart. The process is simple; it is free and independent of the other, you! Remember, the love within you is always ready to open its secrets and share its qualities, but only if you are prepared, sincere, and willing! And here I give you the golden secret: love never aggresses; Silence and Patience are its core qualities. So here you get another secret key to opening the doors of friendship with heart. Remember, Silence and patience are the language of the heart. Ask any 21st-century employer; these are the qualities they are willing to pay fortunes for, praying the institutions to prepare youths for, and if you are thinking, what is so great? Remember, Artificial intelligence can never replace the quality of hearts; machines are not replacing humanity; the heart is the savior! But these qualities can only be transferred from one human being to another, to the ones who are ready to become extraordinary millennials of the 21st century. So, remember this secret for life: the only quality you need to develop to unlock the treasure of abundance of richness within you is the "quality of heart," and the day you master the art of making friends with your heart, you become legendary, you transform, you become the masterpiece! You become love.

Therefore, we all might feel we know love, but whenever I have asked people what love is, they have given shocking reactions: explain love! Are you crazy? They fall short of words; it is obvious because the words are the language of the mind, and the language of love is no mind, "silence," that is why whenever a lover has to express their love, they say look into my eyes! Unfortunately, we have forgotten the language of the eyes, the body language! Language, which 21st-century employers are looking for youths to be ready with from day one in the workplace. Are you ready?

Love And Let Love Do

So let us get closer to real-world success together and see how being in love or being with your heart as opposed to being in the mind can make you a far more successful professional and a human being, the legendary.

You must have heard of this famous quote, "Do what you love or love what you Do," if you get inspired by the above quote! You have made my efforts successful because love is the constant here either way! I might surprise you, but this quote is wrong to me, not because of meaning or anything but because it stresses doing! not on love. It is using love to succeed, and you see 80% jobless and 80% of businesses shutting in the first year; the power of motivational speakers! So, to me, the quote should be, love and let love do! And you will be amazed to experience that you will end up doing what you love, and God is love! So, remember this secret for life: when love becomes doing, it becomes an act of God and the reward; love knows no boundaries, entire existence is love, no one knows the end, no one knows the beginning, and abundance is its limits. Remember, love makes the ordinary into the extraordinary, a man and a woman into a legendary. Love is the power; you are the power; you are love; you are legendary; it is just that you have forgotten; I am simply reminding you so you can regain your kingdom, the kingdom of God.

So, we are getting closer to understanding the deeper relationship between love and what we do. Here, I want to give you a little work: think of all possible inventions that have transformed humanity and study a little about the lives of men and women behind those innovations. For the first time, you will experience a miracle; you will see that while they were from different continents, the innovations took place in different time zones and fields, yet something is familiar! All the inventions that have transformed humanity happened not because they were rich; most were from low-income families, a few with broken families, and no money for education and degrees. Still, they went on to transform humanity; how? Existence worked through them! They were the chosen ones. The immediate question that might come to your mind is, where is the love here? Simply existence worked, then why not me? It must have been their effort. So here I say, while the above questions are genuine, one unquestionable truth is that their education had nothing to do with the inventions; education was not the catalyst; it was an existence that was the common catalyst, and that is the focus I wanted to bring it to you, so it becomes your understanding that all inventions that have impacted humanity, all businesses that last for centuries, their innovators, their founders had very little education, few were dropouts or with great difficulties they completed their degrees and why I wanted to bring this to your attention is, so your mind can become little open, so that question of mind the survivor disappears. Of course, it will take time for your mind to accept existence, to accept heart, but you will see education has absolutely nothing to do with transformational changes that impact humanity; education never was and will never be the catalyst of change because only the master can create original, enslaved people follow. So, when you read about the lives of the legends, you will know without any doubt that existence is the supreme master, the transformer, and whoever is friends with existence, in love, existence expresses through them, they become the medium, they become legendary! To make it easier for you, I have shared the brief life story of three men who, through their works, have created an indelible impact on humanity. Please read them as we continue the journey together. I promise you that it will enrich you, and your mind will become flexible enough to accept that real success is of heart so that this new knowledge can find its way to the heart; that space is called no mind! Where else will the mind go? You are the master; your mind follows you wherever you go! Be aware! Awareness is the golden key, the only quality worthy of education.

God is Love. Love is God.

Love. Love. Love

Transform Inside Out

With examinations, it comes to my mind: why should only teachers have all the fun? Remember, I have said before, by no means am I telling you to quit your school or college, become a rebel, and become part of the problem. Instead, my purpose in introducing you to heart and love is for you to become a wiser youth, a wiser human being, irrespective of age, degree, and academic background. Once you have learned the art of making friends with heart, you will experience a miracle; now, everyone needs you. Why! Because everyone is running for love, expecting love from others! And the miracle is you found it within, within you, abundance; you can give! Can you feel your transformation? You have what no one has, the ultimate wealth, which is the essence of all human beings doing, running, and achieving for love, for the kingdom of God, and you have found the kingdom within! You are the richest; you have become the emperor, and what did you do nothing! Just you dropped the apple! You chose to run your race; you became empowered! For the fun part, hold for some time!

The only courage is to be what you want to be.

Enquire. Challenge. Face. Win

From Hopelessness To Hope

There will be numerous inventions in the history of humankind because men and women are thinking minds, and we are searching for a better tomorrow! We all know tomorrow does not exist; it is either now or never; isness is the core of existence! But men are taught to make the impossible possible because we are born miraculously! So still, we are hopeful. Otherwise, we will all be called hopeless people, a society of failures! Can you see the reality, hopeless, hoping?

The point I am driving here is the men who were the original innovators, the transformers, the legendries, their inventions had very little to do with degrees, with the wellbeing of their families, many were school dropouts, or with gap years, health issues, and the one word that defines them, they were exceptions to the normal, to the society and I say it with my little experience of life, the only ones who live by exceptions becomes transformers, the technical definition of an entrepreneur is the one who lives by exceptions! The calamity is our entire education is about following norms and rules! And no wonder 80% are jobless, and 80% of entrepreneurs fail within one year. That is why, for centuries, we have not seen transformational changes because our minds are programmed to follow the rules, textbooks, exams, and success! And a follower is as good as an enslaved person; can an enslaved person even think of his own? What to say about innovation? Can you see the truth yourself? The whole of our education is the education of slavery.

So let this fallacy be settled within your core that with the current degrees and certificates, there is any possibility of you living a happy, healthy, wealthy, peaceful, and harmonious life unless the follower is programmed to become the master, the original to say unless education is changed or you change, ask me the choice, I say no selection, the second is the only option, it is your life!

So, my whole effort so far is to let you see that current education is the education of hopelessness, so your mind accepts and becomes open to be re-developed as a new one, and opens a possibility for a new man, for a new woman, the transformer, the legendary. Having traveled together so far, you may realize that a flower of real hope is blossoming in your heart for the first time, waiting to open to share its fragrance. You are getting ready to be the change maker; you have dropped all expectations; you become exceptional, the legendary.

It Is The Question Of Your Life

So, here I give you the most powerful and most straightforward of all techniques; today, you must ask yourself about the "purpose" you are spending your precious time in school or college, and if you can do this simple technique, remember you have taken the first step towards becoming a 21st-century legendary professional, how? I will share the execution in due course. If you have understood the secret already, you must celebrate; you have the golden secret and the power to transform. The beauty of this technique is that purpose is not the focus; quality is the focus; remember, quality matters! For the first time, you will realize the power of asking quality questions. I ask this one simple question to yourself: try finding an answer. You will not get it; it is the first time! You must explore, discover, discuss, and then arrive at your conclusion based on your own experience. Yes, there is a technique you can get by yourself. No one is needed, but that would be too much to begin with, so I suggest each child aged fifteen years and above go to school and college; ask and settle with this question: Ask unless you get satisfied! If no one can satisfy you, no worries! Listen to your heart; it says I am with you always.

So, you might encounter suggestions, such as teachers saying not to become too bright for your age! Just focus on what I am teaching! So, you can get better marks than others, "The snake. "The parents might say, too early to ask these wise questions. You are a kid! Just go and study; exams are coming! Though I must say, 21st-century parents, like many of us, have become more conscious and liberal about our children's feelings, so chances are that your parents might be delighted with your question and help you find your purpose in education, so your rest of years gets spent wisely, productively, joyfully. Can you feel the thrill? You found your purpose, and your heart is dancing in joy! Here, you must remember the eternal truth told since time immemorial to all sincere enquirers: one question, one idea can change a life; I add one quality question can transform an ordinary man or a woman into a legendary, the golden secret! Quality matters!

The calamity is that the entire education system is against questioning, against enquiring! Macauley devised this education system so cunningly that the power to question gets suppressed slowly, and by the time a child becomes a man or a woman, they become perfect enslaved people with no power to examine, no power to challenge, the root of being a human; an individual gets cut. Can you see the most profound harm the British did to us for enslaving us?

Here let me share with you a secret: the entire education of our country when we were the global superpower, be it wealth, human consciousness, civilization, the quality and standard of life, science and technology, spirituality, arts, philosophy, human empowerment, etc., in those times the fundamentals of the education system was based upon "enquiring, " asking, "the purpose of life" remember very well, I have just told you to ask only the purpose of going to school and college, the very basic, and there were masters who would answer! Can you see the beauty of that education system based on inquiry? And we were the global superpower, the land of humanity, one Bharat, great Bharat!

It would be impossible to name the kind of advancement our civilization has had, the sort of warriors, the kind of artists, musicians, scientists, spiritual masters, kings and queens, princes and princesses, businessmen and women, the wealth we have had, that is why our country was called the "Golden bird. "

So, if the statement that we are nothing but our minds is true, then it is proof of what we were; the golden bird was because of our education, and the golden secret was to ask, to enquire, to question! The end was finding yourself, your ikigai, and your purpose, and let me tell you, unless you know your purpose, all so-called success is just an illusion. It feels like it is, but it remains to be living in tomorrow. Tomorrow does not exist; tomorrow is the creation of all hopeless, educated degree-holders! And this is the disaster education has done to humans, teaching us to live tomorrow! That is why I love the way lord buddha used to tell his students when they used to ask who they were! And their purpose of being human. Lord Buddha used to say, you are that Tatvamasi - Come. Sit. Watch and realize. His whole of teaching was this process, the outcome of which was self-realization, finding one's ikigai, one's purpose in life; for some, it takes a moment, for some days, for some months, and some years, and the moment one realizes, education is over, go home! And as far as I know, most of Buddha's students used to live not in homes but in palaces!

Can you feel the beauty and the heights of brilliance our masters had touched? That is why when you are in the job your boss "kisses"! Often, or if you are a startup founder, you kiss your employees more! Be alert; I am watching your thoughts! It is to say, "Keep it simple, stupid"! Education has complicated our minds for centuries, and we are trying to simplify life by applying our thoughts. Someone has said it, so straight men as is, is useless. I mean, used-less! So, there is an urgent need to do more use more! Pull up!

Here, I remember an actual incident: the experience of one of humanity's most remarkable scientists, "Einstein." He had said during his childhood days when he went to school and returned home, unlike the regular mothers who generally ask their children, how was your day? How was the class, how was the teacher, how much did you score, what did you play, you eat, you like, feeling hungry! And many other such questions, in which you can see the usefulness! Of course, in love, one wants to know everything about the lover, and the lover is never interested in the quality of the ask; the lover is always interested in the quality of attention they get! That is the chemistry of love!

But "Einstein," says his mother used to ask something very peculiar; his mother used to ask him, "What did you ask from your teacher today? If you have been with me sincerely, I have already given you the golden secret to success, to become legendary! Einstein is the proof, and you cannot say I do not know or have not heard of Einstein! And by any chance you have not heard of him, next time you open your refrigerator, remember Einstein sitting Inside! So, Einstein's life is just one of the examples of how an ordinary child like yours and mine goes on to become one of the most outstanding scientists ever born on earth simply by enquiring and asking quality questions! and that education came from his mother, at home out of the school!

So, by sharing this incident, I am not saying you should start doing the same with your child! We are living in the 21st century, so even if I request to do so, most likely when the child returns from school, the mother won't be at home, busy solving the problems of tomorrow. So do not worry; I am not here to create a conflict in homes or disturb the rot learning ways; it is already rotten, and I do not want my hands to get dirty.

Did You Know

According to popular lore, Albert Einstein was a poor student. Indeed, he did not earn top grades in every subject, but he excelled at math and science, even though he skipped classes and had to cram for exams.

Reference article by the American Museum of Natural History

But I request that you develop the courage to ask, do not think what others will think, and remember others are snakes, born to throw you out of heaven; let others go! But remember to ask in a manner that does not make your teacher feel like a fool and that you are intelligent. Remember, this is the first step to humility; it begins by respecting the person you acquire knowledge from. Calamity is that for a long time, no one has been going to school or college to gain knowledge; everyone goes to earn a degree, a piece of paper! And the disaster of all disasters is the process of inquiring or examining is also reversed! Master is asking a question! The exam is the word, the origin of which comes from examination, which is another name for enquiry. Can you see the calamity? The one who is supposed to answer is asking! from whom? Those tiny little innocent children, the youths who came to school and college to enjoy, play, and express their growing hearts, to enquire about the purpose of life so they can write their own story.

So, if one thing I must call inhuman, it is this process called the exam; it has killed the very original foundation of education, "which was a student asking the master"! Now, can you remember what I said? Why are teachers having all the fun? So, in such a cunningly designed education system as Macauley's, you may find it difficult to ask what you want to ask. Here, I want to tell you with all authenticity that you are the child of existence; your mother, the existence, is listening to you, answering you every moment; it is just that someone has to guide you on how to listen to the mother, to the existence, and once you get the knack of listening to existence and your heart, I guarantee you become the master of the universe, the master of your destiny.

As we move together, you will know the secret of listening to existence, and for the first time, you will experience the ultimate miracle! The one asking is answering; the other is an illusion, Maya. You will experience that existence is not outside; it is within you; you are not separate from existence; you are existence; alone, you are enough!

So, while it might still sound philosophical and complicated to find your heart, to understand the feeling of love, the language of love, the power of love, listening to its existence, the simplest of all understanding and all secrets is the power to ask. And no one can say it is difficult to understand "how to ask?" because day in and day out, everyone is busy asking the other. What! A food for thought, any guesses?

❖❖❖

Specific Is Terrific

So, I will take you into the real world, where everyone is busy asking! But no one seems to be getting what they want! In the real world, you might be seeking a job, working but not happy, not being able to grow up in a career, or you might be an entrepreneur, working hard, burning the midnight oil! But you cannot make ends meet; loans and liabilities are piling up, sales are not increasing, profits are not growing, but body weight is increasing, and you are seeking help from spiritual masters, mentors, coaches, friends, and family. You realize everyone is busy solving the problems of tomorrow! Then, at last, you think of God and the poor God! he is just waiting for you to ask! And he is answering! But have you learned the art of listening? And because you cannot hear, you say, there is no God! It looks like the man and the woman being judgmental begins with God.

So let me tell you, the root cause of all your problems is that you behave like that mother in love with the child, simply asking! So, while millions of youths are running to become Einstein, I am giving you a crazy suggestion: You become the mother of "Einstein"! Drop the apple; run your race!" With this simple technique, 80% of your problems will disappear if you feel you have one.

But I also know that even though I am giving you the simple technique, you will not believe it because your mind is tuned to make simple things complicated, so the IT professionals get jobs to apply thoughts and develop machines to simplify life tomorrow.! So, you need to trust yourself, which is possible when you live in your heart! And if you have been with me, you know how to be in the heart! You have become trustworthy! You have become that, one in a billion, the reliable, rich outside, richer inside. Ask a legendary business person what quality they look for in leaders to run their business empires! Any guesses?

You Are ABorn Legend

So, as the first step, whether you are studying or already in a job, running for a career, or running your startup, remember that the key to becoming ahead of the crowd is learning the art of asking quality questions and listening to your heart. If you contemplate it, this one sentence alone will tell you that you have found the secret of becoming the extraordinary millennial of the 21st century.

The next thought would be asking quality questions and listening to the heart. So, my focus now will be to take you to a point where just by being with me, you get your answer, or just by little practice, you get it; it depends on how sincerely you are with me, from my side, know that I am totally with you always.

So, let us explore how to ask quality questions! Please pay attention; here, my thrust is on quality rather than asking. So, to ask quality questions, first, you need to know what quality means, and, at this moment, if you have been with me sincerely, you will remember your heart! So, heart or love is the origin of the word called quality, which is why teaching love to every child is essential. Sounds like crazy! Quality, heart, and love! Such a unique relationship! But then, the real transformers are always exceptional and crazy. Check it yourself; this is an eternal truth.

Here, I must refer to a few quality systems such as Iso, Lean, or Six Sigma to help you understand quality. Again, please pay attention; my focus is to tell you that quality is a system; it is not an object but a subject! You must be aware in the real world, the most successful companies have the most stringent quality systems, and you will agree with me by this logic: There is no more successful company than existence, and its quality system, working for eternity, has never failed in managing and creating miracles! Let me tell you, an enlightened master has said God is neither a man nor a woman; God is a quality! And I have heard God expelled the man and woman from the heavenly garden because they ate an apple! How about saying God removed them from heaven because they bypassed the quality system? It does not matter if the snake ignited to taste! The real world is not about who; it is about you! So here I am sharing a golden secret: quality is our life force; it is because of quality we, the men and women, are alive and kicking; it is the quality because of which two people start a business, one goes on to become a legendary and another struggle to survive. It is due to the quality of two people starting a career; one becomes a CEO, and the other remains a clerk. Now you know it is the heart that reflects the quality of existence and look at the calamity entire education is of mind the non-qualitative, non-existential, nothing of heart, of love and here let me share a secret that can transform your life here and now, the secret behind why a country goes on to become a developed nation and another remains a developing or a backward country, it is the quality of education, it is the education of inner, of consciousness that makes a country a great nation and this is precisely the reason our country was a golden bird because the whole education was of developing inner qualities, existential qualities, of expanding consciousness. The education of which Macaulay cut the roots; yes, it is correct, there was no other way to enslave us, we the glorious human beings. So, if you want to become legendary, the master of your destiny, you have the secret key: take a leap of faith and jump into your heart.

May through this book you develop the qualities of heart, the qualities of love, may you become love, the one in billions the world is looking for, the new man, the new woman.

"Tatvamasi - You are That."

Original. Incomparable. Masterpiece

Best Is Not A Competition; It Is A Quality

Ever thought, for one goal, for one purpose since eternity, men and women, eating an apple and running, what does it mean? What is the meaning of best? Just think for a moment: if it was not the school or a college, would a child ever even know that someone superior or inferior exists, that someone successful or unsuccessful exists? You can check with anybody, except in the premise of a school or a college; nowhere in the universe are two compared! There are animals, trees, rivers, mountains, stars, the sun, and the moon under one sky; all are happy, enjoying, dancing, eating, mating, loving, living in original resorts and heaven, in harmony, everyone helping each other grow, becoming more beautiful, and look at we the degree holder educated men and women, so jealous of even animals! To make a personal home in a resort, killing all that is so beautiful, in total love, in harmony with existence, so innocent that they do not even know an enemy called human exists! So, instead of identifying, igniting, and nurturing each child's existential qualities, the education system of Macaulay has destroyed the foundation of the possibility of developing a unique, original, loving man and a loving woman in tune with nature, just like animals! What an irony! Men and women have been better than animals because they can think and have minds! Can attain the knowledge of the supreme, of love, of God! Any guesses on how much we, the educated degree holders, have fallen?

You may wonder then what the meaning of best is and how to become the best without running in the race! So, in the education of the heart, understanding the definition of best is essential, and it is as simple as the heart, unlike that of the mind. So, in simplest of words, the best is a quality; it is a feeling; if you think over it for a moment, all running will stop in this very moment because feeling and quality are our treasure, our power; it is existential, we are born with existential qualities and remember when the master says God is a quality, means another name of existence is quality. How can one divide the existential quality? Reality is one, which is why it is true: we are all born masterpieces. We are all one. Not only we, the humans, but the animals, the trees, the sky, the earth, the mountains, the rivers, the sun, the moon, the stars, the flowers; every creation is shining and singing the glory of existence in their ways, except the men and women! What has happened? We ate the apple, went to Macaulay's school and college, learned running, and got lost in cutting throats! The mother, life is waiting for us to return; it has been centuries since we have lost our way home. We have gone too far away to kill.

From day one, a child goes to school and, till the last breath, must run for Success; we have no choice; we have eaten an apple; it is in our blood, and the innocent child knew nothing about the apple; they ate because the other "the snake" told, and it has been centuries everyone is asking for other's blood! Because the other, the snake, is enjoying in heaven! And we, the innocents, are thrown to hell!

So, if you can see, deep down, everyone is running to kill the other and get back to heaven to regain their original home, their kingdom, so what if we have to kill the other? After all, the other is responsible for our misery! And everyone is afraid that if someone from hell reaches first and kills the other, they will miss heaven! Fomo, you see! And thus, the birth of the "race" means to run faster than the others, to kill! And the ones who cannot kill more quickly are called failures, unfit, and defective. Are you getting the clarity? How education is fooling us! You can now feel men's situation, either keep running to kill or sacrifice; another name for this race is the mad race! And the women! It seems they have taken a back seat; remember, there is a woman behind every successful man! Are you thinking otherwise? Go on!

So, let the heart be your only education, the only goal. May you always be with your heart, with your best companion, and remember for life that home is where the heart is, your kingdom is, and you have never lost! It's just that you have been running in the wrong direction!

May this book help you build your path and start your journey! Remembering the famous quote, "Success is a journey, not a destination"!

Life is an opportunity.

Experience. Quality. God

Experience Is The Only Way In And Out

I am sure you got the answer to your fundamental question about being the best without competing with others! And you are satisfied! If not, no worries; we have a long way to travel together. I will do my best to satisfy you. The immediate question might be, how do you learn and develop the qualities of the heart?

Let us get to the point; I have two ways to answer: one is like a motivational speaker, which is like, yes, you can do it; you need a push! Push and be your competition! There are millions of motivational speakers ready to motivate you to do! For free! Why me?

My way is the way of life, which you can relate to, which can become your own experience, and as I said before, what becomes your experience remains with you for life; you become that! The experience reminds me of a short story; see if you can relate to your question, and then we will move into the question again for an answer.

The Life Of A Seeker

A disciple wanted to know what life is. He went to many masters; some said it is like a canvas, some said it is like an emptiness, space, some said it is full of colors, but the disciple was not satisfied! One day, the disciple was passing by a forest. It was late in the evening, and it seemed wise to take shelter for the night and resume in the morning, but it was a forest; rare was the possibility, but that seemed to be his night! he walked about a mile further and saw a small beautiful white hut covered with a red pyramid-shaped rooftop, a candle glowing, spreading the rays through the small window. The disciple could not believe it was for real! His heart was delighted, seeing the hut itself; it was clear that it would be of a mystique, and that feeling added to delight because, tonight, he might get satisfied! So, he walked towards the hut about five hundred meters away and gently knocked on the door. A melodious voice said the door is open; come in! For a moment, the disciple got lost in the melody of the voice! Please do not wait; it is time; I must sleep; the voice came again! Disciple, as if he woke up from a dream, quickly removed his footwear and pushed the door to enter; mind your head! The voice said; the disciple bent a little and entered the hut, and for a few moments, his eyes went blurred as if he was sleeping, and suddenly someone turned on tens of tube lights together! He could not see anything, and with his eyes closed, he bent on the direction from where the flash was coming; how can I help you? The mystique asked. The disciple looked up and opened his eyes gently, and as he had thought, he saw a mystique! cladded in a pure white attire with a white shawl, an aura so magnetic that one feels like it is dissolving. He was in awe, and the mystique smiled and gently asked again, what do you want?

With great difficulty, the disciple could say, kindly allow me to stay overnight; I have to go far away; it is dark, and I will leave early in the morning. With a smile that can break the hearts of millions, the mystique said you are welcome. I stay alone, there is enough space for two! I also have an extra bed! You can sleep comfortably, and a shawl is on the hook; please cover yourself. It will be cold at night, and some food is left today. I made a little more than usual, so before you go to sleep, please have it; it will give you the strength to resume your journey in the morning. Now I must go to sleep, mystique said. The disciple was in awe; his eyes were wide open, only looking at the face of the mystique! Good night, and the disciple saw the mystique gently walking towards his room and the door closing; for a few moments, it felt as if he was immersing in the coolness of existence and a layer of golden light was covering his entire body, giving warmth that he was in a baby cradle floating with a mild breeze.

And a miracle happened, he heard a voice, this is life! And tears of joy started flowing down his eyes; he got the answer! Which he had been looking for for years, and he slept off. Morning, he woke up very early, bent on the door of the room in which the mystique was sleeping, kissed the ground, gently walked towards the door, and this time he minds his head, came out, turned back at the hut, looked up in the sky, kept his right hand on his heart and with tears flowing his eyes, he said, thank you for the experience and walked away. Since then, the disciple never asked questions; he remained silent for most of his lifetime, and whenever his fellow disciples asked if you got the answer! Tell us also what life is! He will smile and reply, do not ask; experience!

Now let me address the question: to develop qualities of heart, you must know the origin of quality and see if this satisfies you! To me, experience is the origin of quality, experience is the mother of quality, and having known the disciple's story, now you know what life is: an experience. Please understand this once again: life is available within the minutest creation in existence; it would be appropriate to say existence is the whole of life, and look at the beauty, the miracle of being human, is that the power to experience the quality is only with the human beings! Can you see the treasure of knowledge you have got? Can you see now why you are unique, why all men and women are born unique, the masterpiece? And while you ask, let me say not only men and women, even animals, trees, birds, even the minutest of creation in the universe, there is no copy, only originals, and why we, the men and women, are called the best creation of God, because every man and woman has the freedom to create their own experiences, their quality of life. Such is the power; we are born with the energy to write our destiny; how about saying, write our own experiences! A life to cherish, a life to celebrate, a life to remember for life, a life to experience the ultimate quality of life, the God!

So, you can see here that quality is the catalyst; quality is the apple! Did you notice we did not run to kill the snake? It disappeared; we just changed the quality, and the apple dropped! And mind transformed! The destructor became the creator. Therefore, please remember always that in life, quality matters.

I hope you got the secret which for over centuries has been kept hidden from you, so you remain a slave. Now you know life is the only master because life has created you, the supreme has created you; how can you be anything less than extraordinary, the legendary, the masterpiece? You are the best quality, you are the brand, you are the brand ambassador of God!

Can there be more success in the real world than you becoming a brand? How many can achieve this ultimate success of becoming an inspiration for millions to follow, God-like, beyond success? The best to say is success follows wherever they go! Is it not a rarity, one in billions? And now you know why my way is a way of life! My way is the way for you to become a brand, the unique, the legendary. Are you thinking, Crazy me!

You, the brand! Is it so simple? Now you know who to ignore, let go! Change the quality! And you become unique, an exception, in this very moment. Today is your moment; make it an unforgettable experience to cherish!

May you create a life of abundance, may abundance be your destination to travel, may you experience the supreme qualities, may you write your own experiences, may you experience existence, and may you become one with existence? That is my prayer for you.

Life is an experience

Love. Live. Write. Yours

Entrepreneurship Is A Mind Made Of Heart

The last question could be how to experience becoming a brand, meaning how to experience the best of yourself! So let us begin by addressing how to experience the brand YOU, what it takes to become a brand in the real world, without competition, without being in a race. Here, you can experience the beauty of asking a quality question! The ones asking can answer themselves, quality, brand, and competition; you must be joking; that is impossible! So, the question itself drops! Did you get it? Dropping out is the only cost of becoming a brand: rewards! Lifetime and beyond. Did you see why I told you that you have the treasure within? To remind you, the very meaning of the brand is premium quality apple! I hope you got the answer just like that disciple got!

So let us do some thinking now! Please think of the people whom you and I worship as the best or the people who have become brands; it could be in politics, the army, sports, movies, music, arts, dance, singing, business, social impact, or any sphere of life think of them. Without dispute, you will find one thing prevalent in them: they all were or are and will be entrepreneurs! Before you jump to judgment, I am telling you to become a businessman or businesswoman, judgmental hai kya!

One thing you should get clear is that entrepreneurship does not mean doing business; entrepreneurship is a mindset; it is an attitude. This understanding will eliminate unwanted confusion among youths and professionals who want to become entrepreneurs but are scared to take the plunge because of misinformation provided by mindful, well-informed global startup mentors, coaches, and influencers. Every youth on earth has to have only one education: the education of developing an entrepreneurial mindset:" One in all, all in one.

So, you understand that current education is all about developing job-seeking mindsets, or many call it the seeking mindset. Here, this is very important for you to understand; please pay attention; you will know how cunning and cruel human Macaulay would have been, laughing in heaven! In our original education, which used to begin by enquiring, the student who enquired was called the seeker, and the teacher who answered was called the master. The joy of education was that it was purely based on questions and answers, and in the process of Q&A, the seeker finds their purpose in life and becomes empowered and self-dependent. In Macauley's language, you can say they become a master's degree holder, a very diminishing reference, though, but that is what his whole purpose was to diminish us and ridicule our education system.

That was the glory of our original education. The process of Q&A was called "communion," the most beautiful, powerful, and simple way of transferring knowledge to a child, which makes a child the master because they have known their purpose in life and have become empowered. How can one even dare to dream of making an empowered youth an enslaved person? It is the only impossibility! Can you understand? Are you with me? And that is where Macauley attacked, on the roots, and the education of life and heart became education of mind and memory. You can check that education of the mind is condemned across societies because its ills have left humans the living dead, killers, diseased, and orphaned! So, while the seeker and master are still there, the outcome is education doing a headstand; Sheers Asana, the master, is enquiring, and the student is answering. Chaos guaranteed.

I call this education system the hypocrisy of modern independent society. So, it would be fitting to say that the current education produces nothing but enslaved youths; no wonder we are called computer coolies, the white color laborers. Can you see the cunningness of Macauley? No guns, no bombs, no violence, made emperors the beggars, the enslaved?

My purpose here is not to say being a job seeker is good or being a business person is good; let this be very clear: the education of entrepreneurship is all about helping you find your ikigai and choose to be what you want to be, the only true meaning of empowerment and the sole purpose of education.

My intention is to empower you to be what you want to be, the only success in life. In your success, I win.

> **Did You Know**
>
> In our country, **four crore youths** graduate every year, **70%** of them have degrees with **no specific industry needs**. Only **5-15%** people in India have their own businesses able to provide employment to **15-20%** of the total graduates.

It is all there for you to see how there cannot be cutthroat competition to survive, better to say competition to kill; after all, it is a question of life! And what is life, an experience! So, do I need to prove who and why we are the CKOs? Are you still hoping for a better tomorrow? Go on! It is your life; you have the power to choose!

So let me now take you closer to the door and open the diamond secret. Entrepreneurship is the way to experience your best, and I repeat here, entrepreneurship does not mean running a business; Entrepreneurship is a mindset, a mind made of heart!

Now, the question arises: If entrepreneurship is about something other than building a startup, what is it? It is a mindset beyond the textbook, a mind developed by enquiring about life, and life has nothing to do with math or physics. Life has to do with you. Life, the mother, is waiting for you at home, but you are busy solving tomorrow's problems, and it is not your fault because everybody taught you to run for life! Nobody has taught you that you are because life is. A mindset that knows how to live in chaos, an attitude that lives in today as if there is no tomorrow, and a mind that is aware there is a supreme CEO to whom we all must report one day. The surprise call can come any moment, and when the call comes, they exit silently, as if they never existed outside. But live inside the hearts of millions forever! That is an entrepreneurial mindset! The one who lives life!

So, as I said, instead of getting into a rote learning mode and adding to hopelessness, let us experience the learning method developed by our original masters, the question-and-answer method, and here I must tell you, we have forgotten that our original masters were the greatest storytellers the universe had seen ever. I am sincerely trying to rekindle that originality, that beautiful way of the original master answering the seeker. In the process, the seeker finds the purpose and becomes the master, the truly empowered human being.

I wish you to become the master of the universe and write your own story to be remembered and cherished for eternity.

❖ ❖ ❖

The Beginning

So, as it happens in every story, I also have a character, my hero, his name is Kabeer. To introduce him quickly to you, Kabeer was born in a middle-class family in India in a city called Bangalore, which once upon a time was known as the garden city and is now known as Silicon Valley or the startup capital of India. Kabeer also has a sister named Shakshi, the most beautiful girl ever born on earth, his father says! You know father-daughter chemistry! Kabeer's father, Gyan, is a businessman, and his mother, Maya, is a freelance digital marketing consultant. Kabeer has finished his graduation as an engineer in computer science and just realized a few days before that he has no interest in becoming a software engineer! For your information, Kabeer is 86% tile-consistent!

What happened inside the four walls? Ask the IT companies who came for the interview! But Kabeer has decided he wants to become an investment banker rather than work as a software clerk in an IT company! You can imagine what must have gone through in the family, starting from the father's inability to understand the desires and feelings of a growing child to what is wrong if it is after the degree. After all, Kabeer is just a child! So rather than wasting time thinking and asking god, why me? Find a way for Kabeer to pursue his new interest; in the meantime, Maya wants to send Kabeer for a week-long holiday with friends; after all, he has just finished his graduation, is 86% consistent, and is a proud mother! So Gyan, not Kabeer, has been given a week time to find a solution about how Kabeer, who has graduated as a computer science engineer in four years with an unbreakable 86%, can build his career as an investment banker, and any delay beyond seven days deadline you know the repercussion, inside the four walls! Thinking otherwise, go on!

Do you remember the famous quote? It is better to try and fail than not start! Gyan had no option but to succeed; he needed to sleep inside the four walls! Another name for this situation is a mess: the life of an entrepreneur living on the edge! And do not think the people at jobs are having fun. Out, shining glasses, green grass, air flowing calmly, and AC temperature in control, but look inside if you can! Volcanos bubbling! That is why, more than ever before, especially in IT companies, special sessions on soft skills, spirituality, and personality development are getting organized to educate the workers on how to become silent! How do they avoid conflict and be productive, apart from writing, understanding, and upgrading themselves to understand ever-changing machine languages? I mean coding! But nothing seems to be working! IT professionals are busy moonlighting! Now, while I write, the professionals are advised to work much harder for a better tomorrow because problems have become more severe and complicated! You are the only hope!

So, let us see what will happen with Gyan and Kabeer. Can they, do it?

Character Matters

So, the first thing Gyan did after receiving the order from Maya was to ring in his best friend Varun in Mumbai, who is the founder and CEO of V&V, a wealth management company that he founded five years ago after quitting his high-paying job at B&G, where he was managing multimillion-dollar portfolios of ultra-rich clients across the APAC region. One fine day! His boss called him from the US to say that while he was doing a great job, B&G was in bad shape, and to survive; they had to let go of the top ten high-paying executives from various regions! In my twenty years of working with extraordinary leaders, this one situation has been the most painful, and this moment defines the true character of a leader, which is to work as if today is the last day of the office! And when it comes, exit silently, gracefully. Outside, it feels like they never existed, but inside, they live forever in the hearts of all those who worked with them, whom they groomed to be the leaders of tomorrow! They have become their heroes, the brand.

You can only be that which
you are, never anything else.
Once this truth sinks in deep,
that I can only be myself
all ideals disappears.

They are discarded automatically.
And when there is no ideal,
reality is encountered,
then your eyes are here now,
then you are present to what
you are. The division,
the spilt has disappeared.
You are one.

OSHO

So, if at all you thought, brand means a large photo of an actor outside a cinema theater or a politician walking with thousands of followers or a spiritual master sitting on a king-size golden chair and hundreds of followers on the ground. You must change that picture forever because YOU can be that role model, that hero, that brand, whoever you are, wherever you are, working in a small office or a corporation, not working, even better! The mind has free space to get in quickly! or that entrepreneur who starts alone and goes on to build a unicorn becomes rich and makes millions richer!

So, having this shocking life experience, Varun set up his wealth management company. He thought it could be a cakewalk because he had everything: the experience of working with a multinational, owning money to invest, and being born in Mumbai, so starting his own business would be easy, and this is the trap in which even most deserving and capable professionals get into, some or the other way in their life, when they shift, not careers but shift life! Let us see what trap Vrun finds himself in and how he emerges from it.

So, while it was not difficult to rent an office in a pause locality across the Marine Drive area, where he also lived, the reason to rent an office at Marine Drive was not home proximity but because he is going to be in wealth management business so he must be rich first outside! You see! The location of your office is so important, depending upon the nature of work or the type of clients you engage with. I am sure this is not something that you may not know, but what may surprise you is that despite having an office in a posh locality, it became challenging for him to hire the right people because experienced people do not want to work for a startup, does not matter how much the founder has had the experience in the industry, or a good human being they are unless the founder offers an excessive increase in salary which only the companies who private investors fund can do and private investors fund only those companies who are solving problems of tomorrow! Like delivering condoms in ten minutes, delivering baby diapers at midnight, shoes in thirty minutes, ask one get seven ! for trial, I mean. You see, it all depends on the mood of the investor! So when you hear a startup getting money because they are developing an app that will track sleeping hours! Please do not start creating an app for monitoring dreams! You won't get money because you will see investors' dreams also! So, if you are considering building a company to solve tomorrow's problem, investors might not even think that is a problem! For them, delivering condoms in ten minutes might be a bigger problem to solve. What can you do? Nothing! Let go! Move on, search for the other! You always need to find out who is waiting for you to come and pitch!

So, Varun was clear from day one: he was not solving any problem of tomorrow; he was helping clients make money today! Let me share that wealth management is one of the riskiest ventures, and the investor invests only in safe heavens! Investing is tricky because nobody knows whether heaven exists; They invest in hope! Tomorrow, they can live in heaven! And we know the miracle happens!

Did You Know

India has over **1, 12 718 DPIIT -recognized startups as on October 2023. 80%** of startup fails within **one year**. Only **10%** survive beyond five years. Only **One in twelve entrepreneurs succeed** in building a successful business.

The Only Courage Is To Be What You Want To Be

I have been meeting millions of youths, graduates, and early career professionals across the globe, and most of them, about 75%, want to become entrepreneurs; they want to become emperors! But they need to gain the proper knowledge, information, and education. Unfortunately, as the mind is programmed, they feel it is better to be a beggar than to become bankrupt! Can you see why it is right to say that ignorance is death? The irony is that today, a Zomato delivery boy or an Ola cab driver is earning a higher salary than a computer science or electronics graduate; see who understands the business; the ROI is better! Please do not think otherwise; I am not saying that stop becoming engineers; honestly, no harm either; think ROI-wise! So, youths with a seeking mindset will be in serious trouble; why?

You must know we are living in a GIG world; the money each one of us earns is the contribution of millions of people from across the globe, and it's true for people of every country on earth, so while it looks like we are independent, in reality we are living interdependent and interconnected more than ever before ! and this economic model in 21st century is called the GIG economy in which most of the traditional ways of earning money are fast vanishing, the concept of permanent employment, join today and settle for life is quickly changing to use and pay. You will never know in your lifetime how many companies and what types of jobs you will be taking up to earn your living! Severe warning for singles! I mean single-degree holders. Can you see the skills you need to survive in the GIG economy, in which degrees are becoming redundant and human skills are taking center stage? Companies will not give you a job because you have studied at a top college! After all, your family could afford it! Or you have achieved the highest marks because you are a master in rotten learning! Companies will give you work or a Job for who you are when faced with a challenge! In textbook language, it is called HMQ - human management quotient and the combination of business and human management skills are called entrepreneurial skills, the entrepreneurial mindset, just kissing for you!

So, I hope! You can understand that the future of work is more complicated than ever before in the history of humankind, where man, for his survival, has to fight with not one but three other snakes! Man, machine & women!

You may not feel the seriousness of the problem, the criticality, or the urgency to get prepared now! Because you are on a hope pill! But when you leave the hospital! I mean, when you leave the college and encounter the reality or in case you are someone already discharged, experiencing the reality, the hopelessness, my prayer for you, in the moment of despair and darkness, may this book become the medium for you to find the power within you, the power to listen to your heart, the power to create a quality life, the power to create your own experience, the power to write your own story and may you become legendary, and for that what you need is the proper knowledge, the right education of developing an entrepreneurial mindset, and if you are thinking of going back to the hospital again! Just relax.

Remember, my whole purpose in writing this book is to prepare you with an entrepreneurial mindset in a fraction of the time and cost outside the college. Do you remember "Einstein's" mother? So, relax; we still need to travel a long way before you find your original home, your kingdom. My effort is to make your journey a memorable experience, an experience to cherish for a lifetime.

So, let us come back and see how Varun is doing. It has been five years, and Varun has survived! And the secret of his success! The entrepreneurial mindset!

Did you know

50% of successful startups have their founders an MBA. **25%** of unicorns have one of their cofounders an MBA. In India **76%** of professionals are self-employed and only about **15%** go through formal business management studies.

Do you need any better clarity on the mess we are in? 60% of professionals are trying to swim in the swimming pool called business without knowing the swimming techniques! A little delay, regret for life! There is no time to blame the excitement, the competition, or the partner! And you can't even blame God because you are like Abhimanyu, fighting a war with multiple enemies without being fully prepared! And the enemies are waiting for the opportunity to cut throats! Sacrifice is the only possibility, and the universe lost a warrior of the Caliber of Abhimanyu before he could write his own story! Reason, unpreparedness. And let me remind you again: you are running a race unprepared, better to say unconscious, so be ready to sacrifice your life. And remember, one doesn't need to cut-throat physically; running itself is enough because you do not know the finishing line; how long can you run?, blink of an eye, and there is a mad rush waiting to go for the kill. I see millions around me, tired, frustrated, with no choice but to keep running for life! I could not find a better case study for you to relate to and make you understand entrepreneurship is the only skill and knowledge to help you fight and win 21st-century battles in which you will never see your enemy! The faceless, the unknown battles! And remember, no one can run away from the run! No one can escape life; this is an impossibility, and one who tries, I call them absolute, real failure. But you have the power to choose your run. Run to kill or write your own story for millions to remember and cherish for eternity? This life is your opportunity! Make it the experience of a lifetime.

Now, this may sound like I am promoting an MBA course! Yes, it does, but you know how critical I am of Macauley, and I have not changed much! To me, instead of teaching every youth the chemical reactions and geography, which no one knows when it becomes disputed! Or, the social science and moral science, which have no connection! Morality is about inner intervention, science is about outer intervention, and one never meets the other, but our education is the natural wonder; impossible is nothing!

Through this book, I hope you find the treasure hidden within you, become the emperor, an entrepreneurial mindset, and write your story. You may think how! Through my real-world boot camp, a unique program designed for graduates, early career professionals, and early-stage entrepreneurs, making them an MBA class of professionals with an entrepreneurial mindset at a fraction of the time and cost. Becoming an MBA class professional with an entrepreneurial mindset and a brand without going to college at a fraction of time and cost may feel like a dream, but trust Me! It is for real; you are on the most beautiful journey of your life. Many questions still arise: where is the program conducted, how much time, how much money, which university, certificate or degree program, online or offline, demo classes, and many more.

So, as I said, rather than getting into rotten ways of telling you the program's features, subjects covered and motivate you to go for the kill! I want to let you experience the entrepreneurial mindset first. Remember, what becomes your own experience becomes your knowledge; any form of knowledge that is not experiential is utterly false; remember this for life! Now, you will relate my purpose of introducing Kabeer to you so you can experience the entrepreneurial mindset, which becomes your knowledge. In the process of knowing, you become that! An entrepreneur, the original, the masterpiece. You realize your best self, the best version of yourself!

So, let us see what is happening to Varun's business. Did he become a unicorn founder, being an MBA? What happened to Gyan? Did he succeed? An entrepreneurial mindset!

And most importantly, the hero of the story, Kabeer! Could he become the 21st-century successful professional, a complete man, "rich outside, richer inside," and you should find your answers in the process? If you do not see, listen to your heart; it says I am always with you.

So let us come to the present again; Varun, having entrepreneurial qualities, could manage through the initial roadblocks of setting up and running the business, which means generating revenues and managing operations. Remember, everything in a business moves around revenues, which means sales! He could manage business and operations alone because, at IIM, he developed an entrepreneurial mindset, which means facing challenges as they come! Which also means no expectations from the others.

So, having been groomed with quality of heart and mind, a complete professional, Varun could hold on to business. But having worked in a multinational company, managing global clients, he also has dreams! But as it happens with every startup founder, Varun had started feeling tired because he was the company's soul, and soul must be everywhere! Varun also looked after sales, operations, finance, human resources, and employees' dreams! It meant a lot of physical and mental pressure, and it was having an impact on his health. He could not spend quality time with family and friends and started feeling lonely! Remember the famous saying, "At the top, you are lonely"! And because of managing so much alone, the business growth was slowing down; after all, a man has a limit to do! So, he was looking for someone young whom he could trust and nurture to become his company's leader! But he knew it was not easy. It meant opening his clients, giving him additional time in training and nurturing with no guarantee of lifetime association, and getting an NDA (Non-Disclosure Agreement) signed might not be viable because that meant no trust! Small businesses (SMEs) must trust! But he had signed an NDA with his previous company, which meant he could not work with the B&G clients or employees for the next five years! And five years were over. He knew this was the time to reap the benefits of his hard work in the business. He had built client relations that were of a lifetime! Not because he was good-looking, which he is, or disciplined, systematic, and well-behaved. Remember, these are the qualities of a leader, an entrepreneur, a quality of entrepreneurial mind, made of heart! So, the prime reason for building strong cliental relationships was because Varun earned profits for them better than others in the market. So listen to the following as I share, as if you are reading the scripture, and here I go; in the professional world, all good things begin and end with how much profit or money you earn for the company being in a leadership position. Earning means how much sales you do for the company, and earning also means saving expenses! Do you remember that eventful day, discussing salary increments with your boss, not for yourself but for your team members, because you are the manager? And you cry outside the cabin because you must let go of a few fun-loving guys. After all, the company did not earn the desired profits because the managers did not perform! That is the real world; change is the only constant!

If you are an entrepreneur, especially an early-stage entrepreneur, in the business between one to five years, your world begins and ends with how much money you save for your client compared to the other snakes! I mean, competitors! It simply means the lowest price at which you can sell your product or service with the best quality and value-added features, no matter whether you are earning profits! Because we are degree holders, masters in cut, and win the CKOs!

Do you remember that sales meeting with your client late at night because only employees can have fixed times and health consciousness? Entrepreneurs need to be demi-God, available always, pure souls, ready for the surprise call!

So, you are meeting with the CEO of a one thousand crore turnover company who has called you for final purchase negotiation at nine o'clock the night because he finalizes his purchases with suppliers only after nine o'clock in the night because that is the time, he gets free from his work and goes home, just two floors above! But you traveled by morning six o' clock flight because it costs less, freshened up at the airport bathroom only! You do not want to spend money traveling, staying in a hotel for three hours, and paying for twenty-four hours because you must take a late-night flight immediately after the meeting. Still, you can only book in advance if you know when the meeting will end! You will have no choice but to take the flight at any cost because it is your child's birthday the next day and so many others! Guests are coming to celebrate, and you must help in celebration! And finally, the surprise call comes to meet the CEO!

You enter the board room where the CEO and his priest, the purchase manager who had called you a hundred times to negotiate the final price while you were having a bath, lunch, dinner, or sex! , to tell you that your prices were high! And you left everything halfway! Praying to him that there is nothing left to say! And the moment you greet the lord, the lord looks into your eyes and says your prices are high, and you remember the last negotiation call, but you can't even cry because you are the chosen one! And the lord asks you to obey and sign the purchase order below your cost price and says all the best! And you watch the lord walking away, leaving you and the priest in the room together to plan the delivery urgently. The life of entrepreneurs, the real heroes. Through this book, I hope you find the ultimate joy of becoming an entrepreneur, the master of the mind, made of heart.

So here, if you pause and think over the two situations I have shared, you will find the secret of an everlasting successful, happy, healthy, and wealthy life. No other education or degree is needed. Just understand this and find ways to experiment. If you can do it while you are in college, I promise no one can stop you from becoming a global professional and a human being, that one in millions, the extraordinary millennials of the 21st century. If you cannot understand the secret, try being closer to me; you will get it! Ask your heart; it is saying, I am with you always.

So, for Varun, it was the decision of life, either now or never, to onboard someone who could become his successor and take his company to the heights of his dreams. Remember that famous saying: a successful person is the one who makes the right decision at the right time! But no one says from where the proper knowledge comes to know; now is the right time, and that is the power of an entrepreneurial mindset; it develops the ultimate quality, awareness. The only quality worthy of education. So, the question for Varun was, who could be the one he could make believe in his dreams, the one who treats his company as his own, and it was to be all on mutual trust. After all, whoever they may be, they will join not because of the company but because of Varun and his dreams, and I have yet to come across an experienced person, even a fresh MBA, who joins a small company because the founder is a good human being! They join because the founder is a good human being who offers a startup package joining bonus, ESOP, and trains on the job! See the life of an entrepreneur, dancing always!

Therefore, Varun wanted someone who would join him only for him! And that was his selection process, the process of checking heart rather than checking degrees. Rest he knew how to make a Zero, a Hero! And here his mobile rings and on the other side the Gyan says, Tusee kaise ho! chaap rahe ho! (How are you? Printing money!) and the laughter on both sides burst like a thunderstorm; after all, both were talking to each other after three long years. Still, it looks like they were always connected; that is the way of heart, and the famous say best friends rarely speak. Here, Varun gets his dream boy, the Kabeer, a fresh computer science graduate with zero knowledge of finance and wealth, going to be the dream boy of Varun, the man of wealth.

Awareness is the only quality worthy of life.

Self. Awareness. Abyss. Timelessness

Out Of Chaos, A New Man Is Born

Here begins the series of events that will confirm why the 21st-century youths need only one education, and that is the education to develop the entrepreneurial mindset; the golden secret for youths to be successful in the GIG economy, which I repeat is all about managing multiple situations, multiple skill sets, managing multiple relations! I mean clients from different countries with different needs because you never know who will be the next one ready to pay and use! Gone are those days of one job, employer, business, and partner! So, in a nutshell, the GIG economy is all about how to live in Chaos, happy, healthy, wealthy, and the best! And here, if you think I have gone crazy! Chaos and best! Just remember our very own lord, Krishna!

The most authentic example of an entrepreneurial mindset for 21st-century youths and professionals to worship, follow, and get inspired because if there could be one word that fits Krishna, it is Chaos to the extent that he was born in a prison of his maternal uncle so that he can kill him, the moment he is born! His father escaped the jail in the middle of the thundering stormy night and saved his newborn by endangering his life. Krishna got separated from his mother as soon as he was born, brought up by a family who were friends of theirs, where his father left him and saved him from killing! Krishna fell in love with a girl named Radha but could not marry; at the age of eleven years and six months, he took revenge, killed his maternal uncle, Kamsa, and freed his parents from prison. The universe will never see a war more disastrous than the MAHABHARAT, a Chaos of which Krishna is called the architect! And amidst the Chaos, the lord Krishna is born! With all authenticity, I say without Chaos, we would have missed lord Krishna, the most friendly God in the universe! And if you think I am talking about God, think otherwise; I am talking about you! Because it was someone like you, a rich and talented man named Arjuna with a master's degree in archery, to whom, at a point, life became a mess; all luxuries, all accomplishments, all titles, all success seemed worthless, and in that mess, he asked a question, from a friend named Krishna while sitting inside a Rolls Royce Car! (the chariot of billionaire kings in ancient times) and the lord! The Krishna answered! Therefore, if not for

Arjuna in a mess, humanity would have missed the most entrepreneurial God of all gods ever known in the universe, the lord Krishna!

So now let me tell you in the GIG economy, it does not matter which degree you have, which college you are from, how many marks you have, or which place you are from; what matters is who you are when faced with a challenge, the Chaos, and the calamity is the temples of knowledge, the education centers, who were supposed to make you ready to face the Chaos in the real world have themselves become the centers of Chaos! That is why, even if a miracle happens and tomorrow comes, a better tomorrow can never be possible! Unless you ask! Are you wondering where your friend Krishna is? Listen to your heart, waiting to answer today, tomorrow, and always.

So let us see how Kabeer, the innocent youth born and brought up lovingly with all possible luxuries and facilities at home, and in his quest to become an investment banker, gets in and creates Chaos for Gyan and Varun and how they face it to come out winners.

So, the first storm that was waiting to shake up Kabeer was Varun's office in Mumbai; while Mumbai was not new for Gyan, for Kabeer, it could be the shock of his life! Bangalore is the coolest, and Mumbai is the hottest! Bangalore does not have a proper metro yet, and Mumbai metro! Each ride is considered the ride of a lifetime! So, the challenge was how Kabeer would live and survive in Mumbai in a job he had zero knowledge of! And as always in a family, men must sacrifice! So, the decision made was that Gyan must temporarily shift! It is Kabeer's job, and Gyan must shift! Indeed, we are in the 21st century! Because Kabeer would need help finding a home, getting homely food, taking care of laundry, and doing home cleaning, he must work harder to succeed in the field for which he has a passion but zero knowledge! So how can he manage work and home alone? So, the decision was made that Gyan would help Kabeer settle with work and make all arrangements to set up a home so that he is free from home! And target given to Gyan was three months; until then, Gyan must manage his clients remotely, or whichever way it was his lookout, he is an entrepreneur!

Here begins Gyan's adventurous journey to find a home in Mumbai for Kabeer. You know how much fun it is to get a home in

Mumbai. Varun's office was on Marine Drive, one of the richest in the city, and how could Gyan think of taking a home far away in an economical location? It would be inhuman; how can Kabeer waste his time traveling in the Mumbai metro, for that he must walk a kilometer after working hard! So, the home must not be more than fifteen minutes away at any cost because sometimes traffic may also add time! Gyan had no choice; all his financial planning was tossing up, but you know he is an entrepreneur, born to win at any cost! So, having lived in Mumbai and Varun in Mumbai, he could win! He rented a studio apartment, a room, and a small open space called a hall with a small kitchen and one bathroom; after all, he had to live for only three months! It was enough! for Kabeer!

So here the father and son duo are together in Mumbai, staying in a studio apartment, and any guesses, who takes the room and who sleeps in the hall on a sofa? Finding a cook was not difficult; what was difficult was becoming a Mom; you see, a natural entrepreneur changes role spontaneously. Can you have a better case study of an entrepreneurial mindset? So, he had to buy necessary food, laundry, cooling, and cleaning equipment, in simple language, you know what those items are! and he made a meal menu so the cook could make what Kabeer likes to eat because the cook and Kabeer meeting each other will be a dream! It is Mumbai, the city of dreamers, the runners!

It has been a crazy three days! The home is Live, and the client is happy! Any guesses on who is the client here? The duo is now ready for the job! I mean Kabeer! Today is the Day Gyan is taking Kabeer to meet his boss, Varun, who is also eagerly waiting to see his friend and his dream hire, the complete fresher! Gyan was confident that Varun would like Kabeer because Kabeer is a very soft-spoken and silent young boy. Varun knew about Kabeer, but Gyan knew that Varun always liked well-groomed professionals. In the first impression, Gyan wanted to make sure that Varun saw Kabeer not only as his friend's son but as a well-prepared young boy ready to take on the challenges to be what he wanted to be and this is the kind of youth the 21st-century employers are looking for, the ZEN G youths.

> **Did You Know**
>
> 64% of employers hiring freshers say youths are not at all prepared with social and emotional skills, 74% of teachers say that they want to develop holistic youths but lack time and resource.

So Gyan ensured that Kabeer wore black trousers, a white shirt and that grey blazer he got stitched for his college farewell. A shining velvet color Tie looked best on a white shirt and the Titan special edition watch, which Shakshi gifted him on his previous birthday! Can you picture this? A fresher's first day at Job! Groomed like a prince, I can feel the confidence in Kabeer's body language. Here, by chance, if you are feeling what is so great, dressing up! Just hold on to the thought; grooming secrets will open soon!

Gyan also knew Varun was always sensitive to how people smelled! Quality that Varun learned from his boss, who used to operate from Paris! Did you get how quality transfers? Gyan had ordered a unique fragrance for Kabeer from a friend in Pune who makes pure fragrances made of sources, flowers, wood, sandals, etc. On the first day of his son's Job, he gifted this unique fragrance of wooden flavor. Can you smell the air around? By the way, what is your favorite flavor? Fragrance, I mean! Remembering the famous quote, "Love is in the air. "So, on your next important meeting with the boss, it could be to discuss a target not met, a project delay, a client not happy, or employee reduction; try sprinkling the magic fragrance before the meeting; who knows, your boss can smell the Love! It was already eight in the morning, and you know Mumbai traffic; the meeting time was eight thirty, and it was time for the duo to leave.

At this moment, you cannot imagine how the grooming of Kabeer by Gyan will change his life forever; even Kabeer did not know! So, remember only that teacher or mentor is real who does not give you verbal lectures or motivational talk but who shows you how to do it! And when you do it yourself, that becomes your own experience, that is empowerment, and only empowered knowledge, which is your experience, is what indeed remains with you for life; the rest of all the ways of teaching, motivating, and influencing are absolute time pass, does not go even skin deep and fades away as late as the person shuts! So next time you seek help from a teacher or a mentor, let this be your criteria to test the teacher or the speaker; why should the mentors have all the fun?

So, as planned, Gyan and Kabeer reached 15 minutes early today, and traffic could not have been better! Remember, if you start your day as if it is the best day of your life, an act of God! Existence rewards you, making every moment of the day magical for you.

Here I want to share a secret. Have you ever seen the sky just before the sun rises? The sunset, just before the sunset! Today, you must sit and simply watch! If you do this for just twenty-one days daily, before 15 minutes and after 15 minutes, watch! I promise you that while others struggle to wake up, making yourself up will become your religion and meditation. Remembering the saying, "Do not do different things, do differently."

So Gyan and Kabeer had time to look around the office; it was a small ten-seater office but beautiful, clean, pleasant fragrance around; it was Varun's office! And here walks in the man with a loud voice, owe! Khote kee haal hai! (My dearest friend, how are you!) and both hugged each other; for a few seconds, a complete silence surrounded the office, and before their tears could come out, Varun said Yaar bade dino baad mile! (friend, it is a long time we met!), while they were holding each other's hand tightly still, they walked to Varun's cabin, and Kabeer followed. Varun's cabin was the live case study of how design thinking works, small but spacious, elegant, Vaastu compliant, clean, beautiful paintings, small pantry above all a welcoming fragrance was all over the room. Now Kabeer realized why his father made him get ready as if he was going on a date to propose to his girlfriend! Kabeer now realizes what opportunity he has to fulfill his dream of becoming an investment banker. Here, his upbringing came in handy; the moment Gyan pointed his face to Kabeer to introduce him to Varun, Kabeer got up from his chair and, keeping up with his traditional values, said namaste to Varun. He leaned to touch his feet, and Varun hugged him! Varun patted his back and asked him to sit; it was all done! The body language, the body worked! Did you experience the magic?

It was nine fifteen, time to start the day; phones began buzzing, "Markets had opened, "today, markets were on a high! You know Varun was in the wealth management business. You must have heard time is money. Have you experienced yourself or just listened to the motivational speakers? If you have not experienced it, then wake up! It might shock you, but the entire education system is designed to kill time, to make you unproductive to the extent your whole life becomes a waste, and before you say it is too much to criticize, never forget that this is what Macaulay wanted us to become: a waste, an enslaved person not only body and mind but the soul! And our education has not changed a bit; let me tell you, my heart cries when I see youths in schools and colleges killing time, unaware! For twenty-two years, unconsciously, you have been killing time, which has become your habit. And you very well know we humans are nothing but our habits.

Can you see the calamity and why I said the centers of education have become the centers of chaos? While I am writing the book, a legendary businessperson in our country has suggested that we all Indians must work for longer hours because India has the lowest labor productivity among major economies worldwide. Please know my intention is not to blame you; how can I even think of that? You are innocent, unaware that you have eaten an apple. Unawareness has become the way of your life! The snake is responsible! Who! Now you can choose. You have got the power.

That is why whenever I see motivational speakers lecturing on how to manage time and poor youths making notes, memorizing, and using sticky notes to wake up on time, eat on time, sleep on time, and set timelines, my heart cries! Same unaware youths, not knowing Macauley, the heavenly ghost following them everywhere, he has the power to change faces. So, wake up! Become aware, the only quality, the only power which can cut the roots of slavery, the only power realizing which you become the master of your mind, power with which you find the treasure of existential qualities hidden within you, remember existence knows no failure, another name of existence is perfection, timelessness is its very nature, it is your authentic nature. Just you have forgotten because your mind is only thinking of apples!

So, drop the apple, and you see the miracle; you see yourself, the original, the masterpiece.

Through this book, I wish you become aware and experience the perfection hidden within you, the only quality worthy of life.

Did You Know

India is ranked sixty-two, in the list of countries by labour productivity per working hour, in the year 2019,

Source: Wikipedia, GDP per working hour (2017 US$PPP)

So, coming to present, Varun called his wealth manager and gave instructions to book profits for clients, ordered reception for two coffees, and asked his HR executive to introduce Kabeer to the office and the rest of the team and complete the joining formalities. At the same time, both friends started pondering over how to begin! Which role does Kabeer fit the best? What do you think? Which role suits Kabeer the best? To me, it is sales! And if you thought so, well done. But your reason for thinking could be different from mine, which is my intention, but certainly not because he had to become the next Varun. Here, I have listed why and who should choose sales as their career and see if your thoughts match mine. If none is matching, no worries. Ask your heart; it is saying, I am with you always.

Love is the only hope.

Darkness.Love. Light

Who Should Choose Sales As Career?

- It is recommended that every recent graduate, regardless of their degree or academic performance, should work in sales positions for a minimum of two years after completing their degree. Additionally, they should complete a six - months project or internship as a sales executive before obtaining their final degree certificate.

- Early or mature career professionals seeking leadership and client-facing roles for long-term career growth and sustenance.

- Professionals who are worrying about the future of their skills.

- Youths and professionals aspiring to become entrepreneurs and become successful GIG economy professionals.

The meditation called grooming.

Grooming yourself every morning is the best prayer you can offer to the existence

The Grooming Etiquette

- While medically it is debatable, I suggest taking a bath every day. If you cannot take it in the morning, bathe before dinner, cold or warm, but bathe every day. It helps reduce stress and anxiety, improves sleep quality, enhances body image and self-esteem and provides relaxation.

- Instead of soap, use half a cup of milk in one bucket of water and rub your body and face with your palms; it is the best natural cleansing process. Make bathing a magical experience, an act of God, and a feel good factor is guaranteed.

- Never dress to impress; dress to kill. If you have a dress code in school or college, ensure it is clean and shining. Never wear the previous day's clothes; your body odor and clothes impact your thoughts and feelings.

- If you are a working professional, ensure you shave daily without fail or arrange your beard daily. Your face speaks. Always wear clean, washed formals in the office; clean attire is the simplest way to feel good and adds to your confidence. Your attire is your reflection; shine like no one else on earth.

- Always wear a watch. If you respect time, an act of God, time takes care of you today, tomorrow, and always.

- Always wear clean shoes. Your shoes tell your story.

- Shampoo your hair at least twice a week; remember your hair is in the top position, maintain.

- Always ensure a mild fragrance on your body; a good smell is the simplest way to your colleagues' and boss's hearts! Spread the scent of love wherever you go!

- Looking good does not mean wearing expensive clothes and accessories; looking good means you care for your body. Have you yet to hear that all things beautiful are simple? Your body is Your temple; look gorgeous, extraordinary, or nothing.

- Always arrive thirty minutes before time, be it, official meetings, or socials; you will become a success magnet. Success will follow you wherever you go.

Please treat the above as sacred commandments and practice sincerely for 21 days. If not all, select any three to begin with. I promise you will start realizing a different kind of vitality, a glow, an aura within you like the original flower of the kingdom of God, spreading the fragrance of love. You will become a love magnet.

I hope you got my answer about the sales role for Kabeer. If the question still exists, let me kiss you and say that experiencing sales is the first step in developing an entrepreneurial mindset. Remember, the business world begins with the sale and ends with counting money. Look at some high-pay jargon: CXO, VP, business consultants, mentors, coaches, advisors, strategic advisors, and subject matter experts; who are they at the core? The salesmen and the women, the entrepreneurial mindsets. I wish you to become the best sales person because an entrepreneurial mindset lives to create and write their own story; seekers live to pass by.

**It is not unemployment
which is a major problem;
it is the question of
'unemployability'
which is a bigger crisis.**

Dr. Abdul Kalam.

Trust Is The Only Degree Worthy Of Education

So, the stage is set to launch for Kabeer as a sales professional; it is quite a time; onboarding formalities are over, and Varun asked his HR executive to introduce Kabeer to Vikram as soon as he comes! Before you ask, Vikram is the business development manager, the salesman of V&V! whom Vikram appointed two years before on a relatively higher package because he has eight years of experience in the wealth management industry, and joining a small company was a risk for his career prospects, which he mitigated by taking a higher salary and higher incentives. Vikram was doing well, but the reason for Varun to look for someone outside as his deputy was, one, with Vikram, it was a purely professional relationship. He joined because he got a much higher package than any other company would have offered, and for Varun, it impacted his P&L (Profit and loss). Moreover, as I said, the business world begins with sales and ends with counting cash. Now, the salesperson makes the sales, but who counts money, the CXO! and counting must not be less because that means lesser profits for clients, which means the client may look for the other and you know, the other is a snake, waiting for the opportunity to cut-throat! Second, the relationship was purely transactional; Varun could never feel the personal boding, so it would be impossible to think of him as a deputy because, Tomorrow, if someone offers a higher salary to Vikram, he may leave. An NDA was not in place either, so with him also goes his lifetime of relationships, his clients, so while the association was going on, it was purely transactional, trust was missing, and the fundamental reason for Varun to look for someone outside, whom he can trust. Degree of trust was the criteria! Can you feel anything here? Real success is of heart, never of mind! And here Vikram has arrived well-dressed with a Ray-Ban glass and a shining Rolex watch; after all, his sales pitch to the client is that his company will make them rich, so how can he look ordinary? And here he sees a young, charming, handsome boy, Kabeer, who says hello! to Vikram and shakes his hand. Vikram looks at Kabeer, smiles, and says he will meet him again soon; he has a client call for a deal to be closed today. By then, it was noon, and Varun suggested Gyan go home and rest for today; he would get Kabeer dropped at home; both the friends again hugged each other, and Gyan just looked at Kabeer, waved his hand, and walked out of the office. It felt amazingly peaceful after all the mission Kabeer was successful. Gyan had to make a few crucial calls to his clients, and he got busy with his work sitting at his favorite Starbucks café.

Here back at Varun's office, it was lunchtime. The staff invited Kabeer to have lunch, but Vikram was still on call with the client. Kabeer started getting familiar with all his colleagues about their work, interests, etc., and he charmed everyone, of course, with his looks but also with his composed and calm behavior. It was time to return to his desk for work, and Vikram walked in and asked Kabeer to stay back. While Varun already had informed Vikram about Kabeer's inclusion in the team as a sales associate and made him clear that he is looking at the long-term vision of the company and asked him to cooperate in training Kabeer, in my experience, one area where even best of the leaders become helpless, training freshers! Because training must be done under the immediate manager! You know what it means: threat! Tomorrow, the trainee can become the trainer! The associate can become a manager, depending on how the manager develops today! Ask a fresher who grows to become a manager in their lifetime what horror experiences they go through in the training period; while there may be few exceptions, the majority counts! Remembering the famous quote, people do not leave companies; they leave managers! So, let us see how Vikram treats and trains Kabeer. Could Vikram be the rare exception and true leader like his boss Varun? What do you think? Keep this as a food for thought.

After a brief talk, Vikram had already seen Kabeer's profile: a fresh computer science graduate with a wealth management job! Ask a manager as well, the candidates they get to train, just like two states movie, language differences, culture differences, zero work experience! Coming from heaven, boss referred! So, the easiest way for a manager to avoid trouble is to get away with trouble, either asking for a transfer to another team, saying unfit, a slow learner, cannot cope with challenges, lacks social and emotional skills and if nothing works the Brahmastra, get rid of the problem once for all, give tough jobs from day one, within a week problem disappears. It was the same here; Vikram was to play the Brahmastra because no other options existed ! So, as soon as Vikram finished the lunch, he asked Kabeer to go through the company website and understand the product offerings! And towards the evening, Vikram will meet him to explain the business model! in person.

By now, Kabeer's desk was ready; this is the beauty of being small: things move fast. Kabeer started surfing the company's website, what it offers, and a few clients it has as its premium customers. Since Kabeer is a 21st-century youth, he is aware of all the social media platforms, so he tried surfing that, too. Surprisingly, he did not find the company's presence on some trendy platforms. Wherever he could find, it was just a formality, and as a good student, he made notes to tell Vikram. The phone rings, and Vikram calls Kabeer to say an urgent client meeting has come up and he has to rush; he will meet him first thing in the morning. Kabeer nodded in acceptance and continued noting his observations and what modifications he felt could make the website and social media platforms give a better presentation about the company. It was time for the day, and the receptionist called him to say that Varun's driver was waiting to drop him back home. Kabeer waved everyone bye and walked out of the office, and to the biggest surprise of his life, a silver color Rolls Royce, Varun's favorite car, was waiting for him to drive him home! Remember what I said: start your day as if it is the best day of your life, and every moment becomes magical. Kabeer could not believe for a moment, first day in the office as a fresher, going back home on a Rolls Royce; he got into the car, closed his eyes, and thanked his father! His eyes remained closed, and he heard the voice. The chauffeur was saying it was home. Kabeer had just taken a quick nap in a Rolls Royce; he thanked the chauffeur and walked home. Gyan had not been home yet; Kabeer opened the door, unwind himself, ate snacks, and started playing his favorite soccer game on PS4, which he carried with him from Bangalore. Kabeer was a gaming freak, name it, and he would have played it all! It was dinner time, and the bell rang; Gyan was here, and Kabeer hugged him. Though a little surprised, Gyan knew it was Kabeer's way of saying thanks when he was super happy. Gyan and Kabeer both had been tired. The mission shifting had been wild the past few days, so they both went to sleep.

The next day morning was business as usual. Gyan woke up early; his wake-up time was five-thirty in the morning; he made tea for himself and listened to the spiritual talks of his guru in total silence while having tea, freshened up, bathed, and went jogging. It was a marine drive jog after a long time. Remember, when you make sacrifices selflessly without any expectations, an act of God, existence calls you for celebration; another name for existence is celebrations.

By then, Kabeer had woken up and started getting ready. Now he knew how to prepare for the office and chose the combination today! That is called the fast learner. Gyan had just finished his jog and prepared breakfast for Kabeer, and it was time to go to the office alone today. Kabeer just asked, how, Dad, book Ola! Gyan looked at Kabeer, smiled, and handed him a key; he had rented an electric scooter for him! Kabeer was in awe seeing how much his father cared for him; Kabeer smiled, looking into Gyan's eyes, thanked him! and rushed in excitement to drive the electric scooter for the first time in Mumbai, on marine drive roads. Remember, when you are happy, an act of God, existence dances with you; it is better to say dancing, always, waiting for you to join and look around; everyone is busy searching for God, seriously! Man is a true wonder, and the women are lovely!

The Office Etiquette

- Arrive fifteen minutes early always. Let this be your religion.
- Never leave home on an empty stomach. Your performance, inside and outside, depends significantly on what you eat, when, and how you eat.
- Never Gossip. Remember, the more you pass time, the earlier you pass by time.
- Whenever you complete a job and do not have work, inform your manager that you can take on additional work. You grow when you can do more!
- It's always a good idea to carry your favorite book with you in your office bag. Not only do books make great companions, but they also reflect your personality.

- Keep your desk and surroundings clean, like a prayer room. Remember, cleanliness is godliness, an act of God.

- Having one good friend in the office is better than many for no good.

- Have fun! Whenever there is an opportunity to celebrate, dance, sing, say, write, laugh, smile, or clap, do and do it. Whenever you celebrate an act of God, existence dances with you; remember, God has another name: celebration.

- Always leave on time not only your desk but also your office. If you are getting late, inform at least one member of your family and the expected arrival time. Family cares.

- Before leaving the office, fold your hands, close your eyes, and thank God for the day. Thank everyone you can think of who helped you feel better and work better. Gratitude is the most loving act of God.

Resume Etiquette
(For Fresh Graduates)

- Your Name

- Your date of birth and age

- Your immediate past and current degree status

- Your father's name

- Your mother's name

- Your father's profession

- Your mother's profession

- Your marks (mention separately of all years)

- Subjects of your interest and the marks you scored in those subjects (mention separately of all years).

- Mention why did you like those subjects.

- Your area of interests other than subjects. Mention maximum three.

- Mention what did you do to develop or pursue your interest.

- List the name/s of project/s you did in your college. Project Title. Number of people involved and their names. Purpose of the project in maximum 100 words. Your teacher or mentor's name and what help he or she did to carry out the project.

- Why did you choose the project, be specific, one to three sentences. What was your learning with the project. What challenges you encountered and how you overcame the challenges. Any certificate or appreciation letter for conducting the project, please enclose.

- Can your project be developed into a business.

- Why you are applying for the job.

- What you think you can contribute to the job being a fresher

- Why do you think you could do better than others for the job.

- Any preferences of yours like office distance, timings, transportation mention clearly.

- Activities that you participated, your contribution, how it benefited you and what did you learn.

- Any social activity or a social cause you took up or have undertaken mention the NGO name and about the work in maximum 100 words

- What are you looking from this job? why you need this job.

In The Kingdom Of God, Zero Is Hero

It was the second day in the office; Kabeer took out his notebook book, glanced through the notes he had made yesterday, and waited in fresh excitement to meet Vikram. The phone rang, and the receptionist told him he would be late because he had an early morning client meeting. Kabeer was a youth who knew how to spend his time productively. He immediately took out the book "The Most Important Thing" by Howard Marks, a book that every youth must read to understand that it is not a degree that earns money but the knowledge of how money moves makes a person rich outside. The complicated formulas or history or social science you read in college, thinking it will help you become rich, you may never even use them in your lifetime, and see the miracle when you are sincere and committed to your purpose, the existence writes the special moments for you! Want to see it? Varun just walked into the office asking where Vikram was, and he saw a fresh, clean-shaved Kabeer with one of his favorite books in hand! Can you imagine this magical coincidence? Even before hearing Kabeer's morning greetings, Varun asked how you got this book? And Kabeer said, my dad gave me, Sir, a couple of months before when I told him I wanted to become an investment banker! Varun just remembered that moment five years back when Gyan was in Mumbai, both sitting in the café, and Varun telling him how much he loved this book. He just remembered Gyan as if he wanted to bow to him for being his friend and such a caring father and a human being; in an instant, Varun just came back from his thoughts, patted Kabeer's back, and asked where was Vikram and Kabeer informed him that he would be late due to an urgent client meeting. Varun just walked towards his cabin, but it was already Kabeer's day; Varun was thinking of Kabeer while walking, not Vikram! I heard them say, out of sight, out of mind!

Finally, Vikram came around mid-morning, finished his regular work, and just before lunch time, he called Kabeer to his cabin and told him he had a few crucial calls to make so he would rush him through the business model of the company, knowing very well, Kabeer did not even know what business model means! But that is the real world: run to kill. So, he started explaining how the company manages the investment portfolios for clients, what the commission is, what licenses they have, the different types of subscription plans they have depending upon the kind of clients, and how the product differs from the competition while explaining he kept on asking Kabeer, are you getting it! Poor Kabeer, as if he had a choice! It was half an hour, and Kabeer was feeling like in a cage where butterflies were making humming sounds. Alright, this is it. Go through whatever I have explained, and I will ask reception to give you the product catalog; he rushed out of the office, saying he had lunch with a client. Kabeer, as if walking with heavy legs, walked up to have lunch, which the company provides at a discounted cost, and money gets debited from the salary account, which was optional.

At lunch, Kabeer was silent and blank, and he did not know how to react to what was explained to him by his manager and those notes; he could not even dare to ask. Kabeer returned to his desk and tried recollecting what Vikram informed him about the products, and tears came out of his eyes! He could not understand a word, and he had to sell from next week! But he quickly wiped his eyes and went to the reception to take the catalogs, which Vikram informed the receptionist to provide before leaving the office. Kabeer could understand the real-world protocol and the hidden messages, but it was too early to get in; it was just the second day. Having catalogs now, Kabeer could relate a few of Vikram's points, and he could write his doubts, which relieved him a little. It was time to call off the day. Kabeer took the catalogs with him back home to study further, but he felt heavy. Today, Kabeer was silent; he did not play the game; he was thinking something! Gyan was late today, so Kabeer had dinner and slept before he came.

Kabeer was not feeling excited this morning, and Gyan could feel it. And while Kabeer was dressing up, Gyan just said, change the shirt; not going well, and Kabeer smiled; remember to start a day with a genuine smile, an act of God! The reward is guaranteed! Just that his ways are different, not like your way and my way, the degree way, two plus two equals four, in the kingdom of God zero is hero, nothing is everything!!

Today was the third day; Vikram had plans to windup Kabeer's story in seven days. It was clock ticking, and Kabeer had no idea what was in-store today. Vikram rushed into the office, behaved like he was in a war, and called Kabeer to say there was a client with a ten lakh rupee cheque! It has been months since he has been following up, and it is the cheque he needed to achieve his quarterly targets; the client has asked to collect within eleven, but he has got another client meeting at eleven who wants to finalize the deal, which could earn him additional incentives for exceeding the targets. So, Vikram told Kabeer to collect the cheque and meet the client. It was already ten, and the client was about forty-five minutes away. Kabeer was new to the city and had yet to go out of the office. Of course, Google was there, but his electric scooter may not go and come back, and the battery may exhaust! He had to go by bus or take a cab, auto, or metro, which meant more time. So, the young innocent Kabeer, taking this as an opportunity to prove his commitment to work, decided to take the chance with his scooter and eleven means he had to reach at least fifteen minutes earlier to show the client that the company means business, so where is the time to think! Kabeer had just jumped onto the scooter with Google Maps on, and it was Mumbai traffic. That day, a local NGO was marching to save Mumbai from pollution! And Vikram knew about the green march! It was Vikram's trick, and Kabeer was in a trap!

Kabeer reached the client's place at eleven thirty, and by then, the client informed the receptionist that he would not be available for the whole day; he would be in a board meeting and wanted to avoid handing over the cheque to reception. He wanted to meet the person before giving a rupee ten lakh cheque! You can imagine the situation of Kabeer, a young fresh graduate with dreams in his eyes, given simple work to collect a cheque, and failed miserably, good for nothing. Kabeer tried requesting the reception, but an order is an order; he just felt blinded. By the time the larger-than-life message had reached Varun, the client was distraught and waiting for Kabeer, but he did not reach him on time; many calls were made from reception to check where he was, but Kabeer did not pick up the calls, and Vikram knew very well Kabeer was driving a two-wheeler with helmet and google on, first time in Mumbai, one wrong turn and Kabeer would have been in police station paying fine, so obviously he did not pick call! But it is Vikram who has lost face before the client; it was his client, and he worked hard to convince him to do business with the company; in reality, it was a reference that one of Varun's friends had passed on to him which he gave to his sales manager to convert for the business, but that was the trap designed for an innocent fresher, who has dreams, but no experience, who, to prove his commitment for work, trusted his manager, the educated, the experienced degree holder professional who ruthlessly broke the most scared act of God, Trust ! for what ! to kill and hold power, the position the educated mind at its best.

Kabeer has no idea how he must return to the office and face Vikram and what Varun will do! Any guesses.! Varun was disappointed; after all, he was counting money at the end of the day, and it was ten lakhs' rupees and a client less! And for Vikram, it was a mission to get rid of Kabeer complete in three days, speed matters! So Kabeer came back to the office. It was late afternoon by now; the office atmosphere was grim. Vikram calls Kabeer in his cabin and in a sweet, poisonous way because scolding means an offense, so he knows how to use body language, making Kabeer feel useless being a graduate in computer science, dressing up like a hero, and not collecting a cheque! The peon could have done it! Kabeer's heart was crying; he was unable to bear it. Vikram told him that Varun would meet him tomorrow morning; they had lost a precious client, and the company could not take a risk on a fresher like Kabeer, who could not collect even a cheque; how could he sell? For Kabeer, in a few moments, he felt his dreams getting shattered like a castle made of cards. His mind stopped, and suddenly, he heard the voice; you may go now; it was Vikram," he said in a loud voice because it was the third time, he had uttered it. Kabeer was not listening! Kabeer walked out of office as if he had failed in life! Tomorrow will be the last day in the office and the last day of his dreams of becoming an investment banker.

He came home and looked around at all the arrangements his father had made so he could feel at home, sat on the bed, and just cried and cried and cried until the doorbell rang, and Gyan walked in to see Kabeer in that situation.

Gyan was composed; he could sense something had gone wrong. It has been rare times when Kabeer cried, only if he was hurt deeply, especially when someone challenged him for his capabilities, so it was no miracle for Gyan to understand that Kabeer must have failed on some tasks assigned because of his lack of understanding the business, so he instead of getting in emotion with Kabeer, made two cups of coffees, served in the cups which Kabeer likes, offered a cup to him, looked at Kabeer and asked him, can I help! Kabeer just hugged him tightly, still having tears in his eyes.

For a few moments, Gyan consoled him. He asked him to have coffee and share what happened. Kabeer narrated the incident straight, and it was no secret now that it was Vikram's trap. Any blame game tomorrow would only make it difficult for Varun because Vikram is his central pillar, the salesman. Still, though a bit early for a fresher, it was time to take the game head-on. It is the question of Kabeer's life, and that is what Gyan does best, being a business growth advisor day in and day out with salespeople who think companies won't survive without them. It was a familiar situation for Gyan; he asked Kabeer to bathe. I hate tips, but this one, try; whenever you feel not so good after coming from the office, or from a meeting, or from a place where you did not feel good, take a bath, sit silently, and experience the magic of mood change! An act of God, rewards guaranteed, and here you might be thinking in the morning, Gyan made Kabeer smile, an act of God, but rewards! Kabeer is on the verge of losing his job! Again, God has his ways to reward, and when you are in a challenging situation, he gives you the power to face it, and in your winning, he wins! One can see you winning; no one can see God winning! Remember, God is neither a man nor woman; God is a quality, a feeling, the treasure hidden within you, but one in billions, once in centuries, recognizes the power within, realizes the existence within, realizes the God within, and here I give you the mother of all secrets, the one who realizes, comes to know all success belong to the existence, to the God. They bow down in gratitude, an act most loving to God. At that moment, a simple, ordinary man and woman become legendary!

"From ordinary to extraordinary,
From everything of me to everything of you,

From nothing of me to all of you,
You are, so I am."

Girish Kashwani

It is nine at night. Kabeer and Gyan are walking down after dinner, and Gyan plans to win. Gyan is a master in designing solutions; Gyan holds a master's degree in architecture and is now a business growth advisor with twenty years of experience developing business growth strategies for companies with a turnover ranging from one hundred crores to three thousand crores, each selling different products and services.

So, the plan is that Kabeer will go to the office dressed to kill tomorrow and ask Varun, not Vikram, to give the client's number, and Kabeer will call him! Kabeer was like Dad, are you mad? 4th day, I have not made a single sales call in my life, and you are asking me to talk to a client who is already F**up! Gyan just said one thing, which will make him a winner for life. See if it matches your instinct, too. Gyan shared that in life, every moment, there will be someone out there knowingly or unknowingly doing something over which you can never have control; what is in your control is to think about what best you can do to overcome the challenge at hand and put every ounce of your energy to resolve. You may still fail, but then you would have tried honestly and sincerely to your best ability, an act of God, and reward is assured; God cannot fail, the only impossibility! These words went deep into Kabeer's heart! Did you see when the heart speaks, the heart listens, and now, instead of feeling low, he asked! Dad, what should I talk to the client? Gyan tells him to tell the truth in a way that does not make Vikram a villain, though he is a villain; focus on getting the cheque; again, solve the problem first! Vikram will be resolved in the solution. It was ten thirty by now. Both walked back home, and Kabeer slept in total peace. Did you feel God here, in sleep, a peaceful one?

Kabeer first shaved and shampooed his hair the following day and took a milk bath as planned! He wore his best attire: black trousers, a white shirt, and a black tie with a black blazer as if he was going to chair a board meeting. Guess what he took out? His Swiss watch, which Maya had gifted on his graduation day, and the perfume today was blue ocean! So here in this terrific attire, with a killing look, Kabeer walks into the office, where, to his surprise, Vikram is in his cabin waiting for the first meeting in the morning with Varun. Kabeer walks into his cabin and says good morning! Vikram was looking at his mobile and suddenly looked at Kabeer; he almost fell from his chair trying to get up! And with a choked voice, he replied, hello! And Kabeer knew he had already won the game of body language; remember the saying, well, begin is half done.

Varun just asked Vikram to come with Kabeer to his cabin. It was the first time Kabeer was facing Varun officially! He gently entered the room; he did namaste, an old Indian traditional way of greeting elders, and sat down. Vikram started the same narrative, and Varun and Kabeer listened quietly. He finished by saying that because of this issue, he could not complete the deal with the other client; he could not focus! Varun was like, what bull***? He knew it was like putting fuel in the fire, so there was no way but to burn the house totally, which meant no option but to tell Kabeer to get lost! But neither of them knew Kabeer would give them the shock of their life. The moment Varun turned to Kabeer in a little upsetting way, without wasting a moment, Kabeer softly said, Sir, I have a request. Varun and Vikram were shell shocked, a four-day-old fresher sitting with the boss creating an issue, sitting as if he had come to shoot for a movie and now requesting! Varun, obviously seeing him in the attire, was already prepared to let go of ten lakhs, but not Kabeer! But obviously, he couldn't say it wouldn't be an excellent example for the company and Kabeer, so he asked, what is that? In a confident voice, Kabeer said, "Sir, I can solve this problem; I just need the client's number. I did not get it yesterday; otherwise, the situation would not have arisen. It was googly; Vikram was seeing stars in the morning, and before Varun could have turned his wide eyes on Vikram, he just gave the number, thinking that the client would not listen. Kabeer did not waste a moment; he took an excuse, went to his desk, and dialed the number of Mr. Mirchandani, a seasoned and very well-known industrialist from Mumbai; the moment Mr. Mirchandani picked up the call, Kabeer with a fresh and energetic voice greeted him and asked him that he would need his two minutes to say why he could not come to pick up the cheque on time, guess what! To his life's surprise, Mr. Mirchandani told him, young man, I appreciate your call. Do not worry; I have already told my receptionist to send the cheque to your office first thing in the morning! She told me how disappointed you were being a fresher, first task on the job, and you could not make it due to the green march organized by the NGO, which my trust funds!

And I understand the delay was unavoidable! But because I had an emergency shareholder meeting, I could not call Vikram to tell him that he appreciated the young boy's efforts and that he would send the cheque to his office the following day to avoid the trouble of sending him again! Can you see, it is this quality, the quality of heart, the empathy, that makes a man a legendary businessman! Can you see the feeling, the humility at its best, a million-dollar businessman concerned about a cheque collector's time and effort and the inconvenience of traveling.!

Kabeer hearing these words was feeling in heaven! He just told Mr. Mirchandani, thank you, Sir, for your kind gesture; I am grateful to you; all the best. Mr. Mirchandani replied and completed the call. Kabeer felt like dancing; he won the battle in style. It needs no guess whom, he made the next call and guess what after about seven years, he said, I love you Dad, thank you, bye got to go, he did not let Gyan say anything, Gyan with a smile, took the coffee mug in hands and loosened himself on the sofa and closed his eyes while enjoying his favorite, the café mocha, he won too! Back here in the office, Kabeer was about to enter Varun's cabin, and to his shock, the receptionist said, Varun has asked you not to come to his cabin! Get into the conference room, he will meet you there. A little puzzled, Kabeer took a few deep breaths and walked towards the conference room. As soon as he pushed the door to step in, the sounds of clapping started with the song Many Congratulations, and to his wonder, Varun was holding the cheque from Mr. Mirchandani; it was delivered while he was speaking! Kabeer could not control his emotions, and tears of happiness started flowing down; Varun just came closer, hugged him, and said, " Well done, I am proud of you, Kabeer. You can imagine the confidence and power Kabeer would have felt in that moment. He just bent down and touched Varun's feet, a gesture in our Indian tradition of seeking blessings from elders to do better. It also had a hidden meaning to remind oneself to be grounded, remember that disciple entering the hut, and mystique saying "Mind your head" !, to remember that your success is not yours alone; there are so many known and unknown people who are the contributors to what you call your success, and be grateful to them also, the most loving act of god and bonus rewards is assured, and now remember the smile in the morning and the chaos followed! His ways are different; with a bit of awareness, you can see he wins by letting you win.

It was a day nobody wanted to miss in the office except Vikram; he shook hands with Kabeer, said a good job, keep it up, and left for another client meeting. Guess who must be the client? He would have gone to meet! It was lunchtime, happiness was in the air, HR had unique dishes ordered to add flavor to the joy, and she knew Kabeer likes white Rasgulla, and it was undoubtedly his day today!

Post lunch, Kabeer, now sitting on his desk, was vibrating with some thoughts. He made a daring decision: he called Varun's extension, and as soon as Varun picked up the phone, he said, Sir, I want to meet you for five minutes, and there was no way Varun could have said no today! The next moment, Kabeer was sitting with Varun one-on-one! With the company's catalog and his notes, which he made to discuss with Vikram, the digital media platforms! Varun was delighted because he knew this area needed attention, but Vikram had never shown keen interest. Varun could not afford a dedicated team for digital media management because it was not the core of his business, plus it involved technical understanding of the functioning, which he best left to Vikram to handle; after all, the purpose was to get more new engagements and establish the company as a trusted brand in the wealth management industry, the job of sales and marketing. Kabeer shared his thoughts with Varun, who listened to him patiently. As soon as Kabeer finished, Varun told Kabeer that he appreciated his observation and understanding of the power of social media and that he would think over his suggestions.

Additionally, he told him to share the links of the top three wealth management companies whose websites and social media presence he feels are the best. Can you see the ball rolling? It was the fourth day, and the associate was sitting with the boss, which is the advantage of working with small business enterprises (SMEs).

Today, Kabeer just charmed Varun; for the rest of the day, he was thinking and digging out some of his old files where he had made his business and growth plans. He looked more determined than ever, and it looked like he was thinking something big! Around the evening, he dialed Gyan and said, Tera Munda nu Dil jeet liya Sanu, Kithee ho! (your son has won my heart! where are you?), To his surprise, Gyan was sitting in their favorite hot spot, the Starbucks café at Vile Parle, a forty-five-minute drive from Varun's office, and they decided to meet up. Varun left the office an hour early, and by six, both oldies were sitting together enjoying their favorite coffee, remembering the olden golden days when both were in jobs. They met when B&G chose Gyan's company to design and build the six-floor business center close to Juhu Beach, where they had booked one floor to manage their India operations.

It has been years since they met, and they met forever now. Dasso, Kee soch rahe ho Tusee! (Pl. tell me what you are thinking?) Gyan asked, and what transpired during their conversation would be like Rajkumar Hirani and Vidhu Vinod Chopra meeting to make a movie with the hero, a middle-class boy named Kabeer, who has no idea of acting!

The picture was clear to both: Vikram would not groom Kabeer for the sales role, and Varun did not have time for training! Kabeer knows zero of wealth management, and he must start selling! The billion-dollar question was, who would be the trainer then? So, they debated some ideas, including Kabeer doing a part-time or distant MBA. Still, it was all going to take time and a lot of money again, and whether Kabeer can take it all, or can Gyan take it all, will it not look like that young boy who goes to school and college to become successful and after twenty-two years coming out with no job and no idea where to go and lands up sitting with a counselor taking the psychometric test to clear the mind!

Moreover, to begin with, Kabeer needed to know the business and human management concepts, which, unfortunately, in four years of his degree course, had no mention because he took computer engineering and engineers are not human; they are machines! Engineers are not supposed to manage a business; they are only supposed to do! Work, I mean. So, to even begin independently, Kabeer needed to go through a proper business and human management program; a solo sales program would have been useless without business acumen and human management skills, and let me remind you again, the 21st-century successful professionals will be those who have mastered the art of business and human management skills.

So, the software coding boom in the 1990s, where even a

diploma holder who did an Aptech course got a job in a software company as a software engineer by cutting the throats of engineering degree holders! The 21st century will witness the same boom for business and human management skills; an ocean of opportunities awaits entrepreneurial mindsets, the emperors.

So, ultimately, they concluded that a full-time MBA was out of the question, and Kabeer needed an MBA crash course. MBA crash course! Both screamed together! For a moment, there was silence because, being entrepreneurs, they knew what they had found! Remembering that famous quote, "a lot can happen over a coffee," was an eureka moment for both. Not clear! Hold your breath and watch how an MBA-like crash course is designed over coffee! By two friends who have the potential to groom every youth of India, like Kabeer, with an entrepreneurial mindset at a fraction of time and cost.

Gyan was to be in Mumbai for three months; of course, it was for Kabeer, but he never knew what existence had in store for him for the sacrifices he made for his son to be what he wanted to be, an act of God and remember the reward is guaranteed, his ways are different. You know Gyan has mastery in business growth advisory but does not have an MBA degree. On the other hand, Varun was an IIM alumnus who, better than Varun, would know the MBA use cases and useless cases; remember, 55% of MBAs remain jobless! So, Varun knew how to curate the program just enough for Kabeer to become an MBA class professional and get going with business development. Did you see it? Vikram dissolved in the solution! And Varun knew that Gyan could only be in Mumbai for up to three months, so without delay, he told Gyan, tusee sales training chaloo karo! (You start sales training), because he knew no one better than Gyan to teach Business growth. Baakee mein dekh lenga (Rest I will take care of), you must remember that business growth is not an alternative name to sales; sales is part of business growth. For Gyan and Varun, it was like being young again because that is how they build their teams while on the job, hiring freshers from any degree; for them, a degree was redundant in the selection process. Sincerity, honesty, and trust were their selection criteria, the degree of heart. It was nine o'clock, late for both, so they hugged each other, packed up instantly, and rushed to return home.

Here at home, it is not difficult to guess Kabeer was playing his favorite soccer on PS4 with online friends, waiting for Gyan to have dinner together; it was his day, after all. The bell rang, and Kabeer jumped to open the door. And as soon as he saw Gyan, he hugged him tightly and said I love you, Dad, you are the Best! Can you see the reward? Ask a father when he gets this compliment from his grown-up son; for him, he has succeeded. He just remembered his master, thanked him from the heart for this moment of success in gratitude, gently put his hand on the top of Kabeer's head called Sahasra chakra, an old traditional way to bless the younger loved ones for them to live a long, happy, healthy and wealthy life and kissed on his forehead and a with a smile he just moved to freshen up and, in few moments, both were having dinner and sharing what happened today and form tomorrow onwards, Kabeer will be undergoing the program named Real world boot camp - an alternative to MBA. For Kabeer, nothing could be better than getting closer to his dreams. He was on his track.

Sales Etiquette

- Dress to win in style wherever you go, even on a deathbed!

- Prepare your fifteen-second introduction pitch like a prayer.

- Learn the art of making an effective seven-minute presentation.

- Always carry your visiting cards wherever you go, and keep a few in the car; you never know where you will meet your future million-dollar client.

- Be specific in your asks and gives. Specific is terrific.

- In a conflicting situation with the client, be the first to apologize if it means ending the conflict, even if it is not your mistake, and move on and let go; the act of God reward is guaranteed.

- Before meeting a client for the first time, try to know their likes or dislikes. You never know; your client can become your partner for life, the magical connection.

- Always arrive thirty minutes early for any meeting. Remember, the early bird catches the worm! It is an eternal truth; practice, and you will become the master networker.

- Never cancel a client meeting or call unless you are on a deathbed or in a medical emergency. At least call one hour before and apologize, stating facts for the cancellation; a sure way to your client's heart for saving their time, an act of God, and rewards guaranteed.

- Always check your calendar before committing to a meeting over the call or in person; it is better to be safe than sorry.

- Never smoke before entering a meeting; remember, smoking kills.

- Smell like a flower in the garden of Eden, wherever you go, whatever you do! Have you heard that God is a fragrance?

- Networking is old fashioned; learn the art of making Love at first sight; Love sells. Ye Dil Mange more.

- Never lose a visiting card you receive; you may have lost your billion-dollar Future cash flow (DFCF).

- Learn to be grateful for those who help you make sales the most loving act of God. Bonus rewards are guaranteed!

- Learn the art of business modeling; *The art of doing otherwise.*

- Develop the X factor, be the charming magnet, always ready for the shot.

Introduction To Real World Bootcamp

My efforts here are to give you a glimpse of the real-world boot **camp** that groomed Kabeer as an entrepreneur in three months. While I would love to, it would be overwhelming for you if I narrated the entire session here. So, for your benefit, I have compiled the essential questions that Kabeer asked Gyan and Varun, which I believe are the questions of every youth in their quest to develop an entrepreneurial mindset. I am confident that you will also find answers to some of the questions that you wanted to ask! There still might be more questions you want to ask; I promise you, if you ask with sincerity, you will always find me with you. Thinking how!! Listen to your heart; it says, when I drop you at your kingdom, I will give you my contacts to be in touch for life!

So, for some time, I will take over the stage as if Gyan, Varun, and I are not three but one, the awesome threesome. I hope you can feel it already! So here I present to you the excerpts from the live sessions.

Live Session
Dialogue Between Gyan and Kabeer

What is sales? Is there a definition?

G1: Sale is a process in which one person/s has or might need the product or service that your company has, and you, who could be a worker or the owner of the company, engage with that person to understand their requirements, identify which product or services of yours could fit best to fulfill their needs and proposes the same for their consideration also called the process of identifying the problem statement, explains the reason for offering and the money that they have to pay for using your product or service. The person who engages with people in need (also called the prospect or potential buyer) in the entire process is called a salesperson, and the one with the need is called the buyer or customer/ client.

K2: Is the sales process the same for all the customers?

G2: Certainly not; the sales process depends on the kind of need, the usage, and how the customer will consume the product or service. As a standard, the processes are categorized into three verticals: B2B (Business to Business), B2C (business to consumer), and B2G (Business to Government). A successful salesperson is not the only one who knows about their product or service but has mastered the art of identifying the problem statement. You will learn more about this secret as we go along and will become a master, too.

K3: Which process is easy and which one is difficult? What category of sales process is my company into?

G3: Each process has pros and cons and depends on what kind of products and services a company has and what need it is fulfilling for customers, also referred to as the problem the company is solving with their product and service. Generally, the business-to-consumer (B2C) process is the easiest, followed by business-to-business and business-to-government. Your company is into both B2B and B2C.

K4: How can I start my sales process?

G4: The most straightforward way to start is to ask your sales manager or boss if there are pending inquiries! How you start is the key to your success. I can answer how, but it will be a rotten way, and you can watch millions of free YouTube videos on "how to sell" for no use. So, hold on to this part; this must come from you, and if it does, you win, and we win. The real challenge is when you must reach out to prospects; in that case, there are various ways to get the list of people who might need your product or service, which is called the lead generation process, for which generally companies have a separate department or the company outsource the process of lead generation. Some companies use their sales personnel as lead generators; these companies are a sure shot in the list of 80% failing within one year. Some companies ask sales professionals to revive relationships with clients who, for some reason, have stopped doing business with the firm. It is arduous, but one who dares and succeeds becomes the god of sales.

K5: Uncle (Varun) asked me to search for the top three companies offering similar services as ours and share their website links, and I did. I am afraid they are far better than us, though I still do not know our products, their presentation is fantastic, so why would customers buy from our company, even if I do my best?

G5: So, first, take your time to conclude the end. One quality of the heart a salesperson must develop is patience, an act of God! Rewards assured you should have no doubt about this by now, and since your "How" is pending, have patience; you have not even started, so do not be judgmental. In the first part, Varun asked you purposefully to do so, and you did your best! As I said, the sale is a process, so you have to understand it because the answer lies in understanding the process; the better the process, the better the chances of the prospect making the buying decision in favor of your company, and remember, you are a part in the process, this simple understanding, if you get it right has the potential to make you the best salesperson, you do not need to be an MBA or ten years experienced sales professional! Millions of young and early career professionals who take up sales work have destroyed their careers, feeling they sell. And if they succeed, the company succeeds; if they fail, they, the individual, fail! Which means life has failed for life, the black mark! To me, that is the only impossibility; life only knows success; the other name of life is success, so it was not the salesperson but the sales process that has failed and any company founder who does not realize or accept this fact that a salesperson is just the part of the sales process; eventually, the company will fail! The root cause of why 80% of startups fail within the first years and only 10% survive beyond five years is because the founders lack entrepreneurial skills. Kabeer was in awe! He looked at Gyan, his father! as if he was listening to him the first time. Kabeer, are you with me? Suddenly, Kabeer shook his head and said, yes, Dad! Let us understand why a customer buys from one over the other, which is also technically called a decision-making process. Factors that buyers consider before making a buying decision keeping B2B vertical in view:

(I) How a salesperson approaches the prospect over the call means the first fifteen seconds of the call. Remember, your first fifteen seconds of the call decide whether the buyer will buy from your company or the other, and in these fifteen seconds is the secret of "How to sell," which you continue to hold for now!

(II) Companies' presentation includes catalogs, websites, social media, reviews, and brand image. Building a brand is the most arduous and most rewarding work in the life of an entrepreneur; you will learn about it in the process.

(III) Personal references mean requesting an existing client using your product or services to share their experiences so you can show the "testimonial" to the buyer when deciding to buy. Though I do not want to just in case you meet someone who tries to bully you with technical jargon, the sales process typically consists of lead-> prospect -> potential ->confirmation -> supply -> payment.

K6: What is the secret of the first fifteen seconds of the call or meeting? Can I understand now?

G6: You can! But for that, I will have to take you through the art of making a presentation, and I am sure many of you, when you hear the word presentation, immediately think of PowerPoint slides, and you miss the big time! Remember the secret: you are the presentation, the beginning, and the end! That is the depth and importance presentation carries; often, the slides become a hindrance, and one must avoid them; you will learn the technique, but for that, we will have to role-play. But for your curiosity and the benefit of readers, let me share the essential qualities needed to become a master presenter:

(I) Your presentation is as good as you feel now! Now you know well why you must dress to style, the beginning of the feel-good factor. Remember always, well begin is half done.

(II) How honestly do you believe the product or service you suggest to your prospects will solve their problems? Treat this as a diamond sutra for life; you will be one of the emperors in the GIG world.

(III) If you ever thought that people buy your product or service, that is a mistake. They buy YOU! Again, if you think you mean Kabeer, it is a grave mistake; they believe in your passion, your Love for solving their problem; you know now, they buy into your Heart! And that is the real meaning when you hear the saying, Love sells. Yes, it does. It depends on whether you have sincerely made friends with your Heart so it speaks when needed! Here is the only warning I want to give you: never use Love to sell! Remember always the secret I shared with you: Love is not a doing, so never do love to sell; it is going to be a mess, and look all around you, while everyone is in a mess, salespeople are in chaos, a higher degree of mess! Why? Because they are making a fundamental mistake: trying to sell their product or service! They have yet to learn that Love sells and Love happens; try to do it! Rejection is guaranteed.

(IV) How well you have understood the use cases of your product or the services, and here I am sharing with you the secret which, if you get it, one day you will become the founder of a unicorn, which is what Varun has seen in you today! And to understand the secret, you need not be an MBA or a Harvard graduate. So, the secret is that You need not be a core technical domain expert to be a successful salesperson! It means, in your case, you should have an MBA from a prestigious institution with finance and marketing as a specialization; if that were the case, Varun would have hired many and built his company as

Unicorn or every second company could employ an MBA and becomes Unicorn, the key here is if you have the intelligence to understand the use cases and the degree you need to understand use cases is awareness! and you can look around the most successful founders ever born in the universe many did not have a regular formal education, many were dropouts or having gap years, and many of them had no connection between what they studied and legendary business they built. You can check it, I refrain from making references because everyone is born equal, and can become what one has become in their own ways and style! , the problem, why only a few can become ones on whose names the centuries are remembered, is because of our education, which only teaches how to become a copy; original, transformative innovations have become a rarity simply because education is the education of mind and to develop awareness, education of Heart is needed, lucky are the ones who drop out or escape eating the apple, I mean education! And they succeed in becoming what they want to be! Why? Because when the mind is not, the Heart is!! Kabeer's eyes were wide open! His Heart blossomed like a flower as if he had just been born a new man! So Gyan did mention a few names such as Dhirubhai Ambani, Ghanshyam das Birla, Steve Jobs, Henry Ford, John Stith Pemberton, Mark Zuckerberg, Michael Dell, Isaac Newton, and the man himself, Warren Buffet, and asked him to read the biography of each one because all the names mentioned above are legendary professionals and human beings, remember, you are what you read, hear, and speak! You are an experience! Let everyone experience the best version of YOU!

DID YOU KNOW

College is not right for every person and should not be a requirement for every job. "Some people are going to get a lot out of advanced education and some people are going to get very little". "I don't even think it's important that every person go to a college at all."

Warren Buffet

Brief Life Story of the great scientist Isaac Newton

It is a well-known fact that Newton was not good at studies. Newton's mother, Hannah Ayscough, married the reverend Barnabas Smith and left Newton with his grandparents at age three. He grew up to hate his stepfather and never recovered from his mother's abandonment. By the time Smith died in 1653, Newton's personality had been forged; he became distressful, hesitant in dealing with others, and emotionally unstable; these would be lifelong traits. He failed multiple times, because of which he was expelled from Grantham King School. At the age of fourteen, after his stepfather's death, Newton was taken out of school to work on the family farm. He returned to Cambridge University in 1661. His mother refused to pay for his education, so while at college, he worked as a subsizar who performed a variety of jobs for fellow students to pay his way. He became interested in mathematics after buying a book at a fair and not understanding the math concepts it contained. Newton suffered a mental breakdown in 1675; it took him four years to recover. He then found mathematical proof of planetary ellipses around the sun. Newton returned to his mother's farm to avoid the rampant plague in Cambridge from 1665 to 1666. Without access to his books, Newton discovered differential calculus, which he called the "direct and inverse method of fluxions."

Brief life story of the Indian Billionaire Ghanshyam Das Birla

Born on 10th April 1894, GD Birla underwent formal education only until the age of eleven, after which he followed in his father Baldeodas's footsteps into the family's trading business in Mumbai. In the 1940s, GD Birla ventured into the territory of cars and established Hindustan Motors, India's most loved brand of vehicles," the ambassador" was born. After independence, GD Birla entered the tea and textiles business by acquiring erstwhile European companies. GD Birla diversified his business into the cement, chemical, and steel sectors. As of March 2022, Birla's group of publicly listed companies has a total market capitalization of over $70 billion. Today, Some of the best brands in fashion & textiles belong to the Birla group, namely, Peter England, Allen Solly, Van Heusen, Pantaloons, and many more. India's finest institution with Eminence status, BITS Pilani (Birla Institute of Technology & Science), was founded by GD Birla in 1964. The birla family has also built several magnificent temples in India , showcasing their devotion to the gods and the well being of all.

Brief life story of the Chinese Billionaire Jack Ma

Jack Ma is the founder of Alibaba and Ant Group. He was born on September 10, 1964, in Hangzhou, southeastern China. He was born into a low-income family. As a teenager, Ma woke up early to visit the city's leading hotel, offering visitors tours of the town in exchange for English lessons. The nickname "Jack" was given to him by a tourist he befriended. After high school, he applied to college but failed the entrance exam twice. He finally passed on the third try. He graduated in 1988 and started applying to as many jobs as possible. He received over a dozen rejections from KFC before being hired as an English teacher and earned $12 a month at a local university.

At the World Economic Forum in 2016, Ma revealed he had been rejected from Harvard University 10 times. Though his first two ventures failed, he gathered 17 of his friends in his apartment four years later and convinced them to invest in his vision for an online marketplace called "Alibaba." By October 1999, the Company had raised $5 million from Goldman Sachs and $20 million from Softbank. In 2005, yahoo invested $ 1 billion in Alibaba in exchange for a 40% stake in the Company. In 2014, Ma said he knew Alibaba had made it big when another customer offered to pay his restaurant bill. The customer, Ma, said in the interview, had left Ma a note that read: "I' 'm your customer of Alibaba group. I made a lot of money, and I know you do not make any money. "I'll pay the bill for you. " The Company's $150 billion IPO was the most extensive offering for a US-listed company in the history of the New York stock exchange. It also made Ma the wealthiest person in China, with an estimated worth of $25 billion at that time. As of November 2023, Alibaba has a market capitalization of $217.26 Billion, the world's 42nd most valuable Company. Ma stepped down as Alibaba's chairman on September 10, 2019, his 55th birthday.

K7: Please tell me how I understand the use cases of our services; ours is a product or service company?

G7: Yours is a product offered in the form of services. Generally, whenever we think of a product, we picture an object, something we can see, touch, or feel. But it is not valid! A product could be software; you cannot see anything outside, but it makes the man, machine, and woman run! Remember the famous quote: never be fooled by what you see outside; you never know the story inside! So, products and services are mutually exclusive and depend on the company's business strategy, target market, go-to-market strategy, positioning, and competition landscape, which technically means the company's business model. So, the right way to understand the use cases is to understand the company's business model first; once you know your company's business model, understanding the use cases will become a child's play. I see millions of startup founders with sound technical knowledge and good products but have no idea how to model their business, and they fail. Remember, 80% of startups fail within one year! The secret of failing! So, remember, the business model is like the foundation on which a business is built, and an entrepreneur's destiny is cemented. Varun is the best man and will take you through the business modeling concepts.

K8: I have come across and seen my friends; they hate sales; I love it! Is it because I have got a degree from a reputed college? Or because you are teaching me?

G8: Gyan smiled, and to Kabeer's surprise, he said, it is because you are asking quality questions! Both burst into laughter, and after a pause, he continued, any job is as difficult as you have prepared for it, and that is the only purpose of education is to prepare you for life, and you do for not one or two, but for twenty-two years! Outcome: unemployment, confusion, and unfitness. Therefore, it is a miracle that 20% of engineering graduates can get employment; genuinely brilliant they are! So, with 80% who do not have jobs or entrepreneurial skills, sales will be the most challenging role because an entrepreneurial mindset is essential for the sales role. Unfortunately, education does not teach you how to develop an entrepreneurial attitude. I see youths all around when they do not find any options to get a job; in total hopelessness, they take up a sales job. You can imagine what a salesman or a saleswoman could be without hope! The people we worship, the politicians, the business leaders, the actors, the religious masters; why we adore them! You may not have realized, but we love them because they have mastered the art of selling hope! The hope of a better tomorrow!

So, remember, you love it because you are now getting prepared for an "entrepreneurial mindset." Let me also tell you there can never be a better role than a sales role; there can never be a role as rewarding as sales simply because, at the core, it is an act of God. Remember, only "love sells," which is one of the eternal qualities and the secret that transforms an ordinary man and woman into a legendary professional.

Without a sales person, all inventions will be dead.

Master. Sales. Impact. Humanity

Girish Kashwani

GLIMPSES OF PRESENTATION SKILLS WORKSHOP

SO, WHY ARE YOU HERE AND WHAT ARE YOU DOING HERE

ACTIVITIES
1. INTRODUCE YOURSELF ELEGANTLY
2. THE FIRST STEP TO HAVING THE BIGGEST IMPACT
3. CREATING EFFECTIVE CORPORATE MAILER AND PRESENTATION
4. FIVE KEY QUALITIES THAT A BUSINESS AUDIENCE LOOKS FOR
5. THE UNDER PINNING RULES

POWERFUL PRESENTATION LAYOUT

I'M……………………………………

AND I [DO THIS]………………………………

AND I'M VERY GOOD AT IT BECAUSE

I DID THIS GREAT THING

I WORK WITH

THE FIRST STEP TO HAVING THE BIGGEST IMPACT

* **BODY LANGUAGE**
* **VOICE**
* **WHAT YOU SAY**

EFFECTIVE BUSINESS LETTER

Date :

Name :

Address :

City :

Dear ...

    You are cordially invited, as my guest, to a presentation on "how worthless degrees are creating unemployable generations the way out ". I am honored to be the speaker at this meeting of the Bangalore area, ... and will be covering topics such as why 21st century employers are looking for youths with business and human management skills. Why aspiring and early stage entrepreneurs must prepare themselves for GIG economy in which people look purpose driven engagements than the traditional skill driven models.

    As a member of our business community, I look forward to meeting you and sharing with you the benefit of our real world boot camp an alternative to MBA at fraction of time and cost especially designed for aspiring and early-stage entrepreneurs.

    You will have the opportunity and can meet with other business professionals in your community, enjoy some networking and perhaps explore the possibility of sharing business.

    This special event is on date..., day.... We will begin at (Time) and end at (Time.) sharp. We suggest you to arrive thirty minutes before at the venue.

    I request you to fill up the form as a confirmation of your attendance for us to make necessary preparations. Please bring plenty of business cards, as you will meet many local businesses people.

Sincerely

Girish Kashwani

Founder

Pk Consulting

FIVE KEY QUALITIES THE BUSINESS AUDIENCE IS LOOKING FOR YOU IN

- At ease / self aware
- Dynamic / Dressed to win
- Sense of purpose / in charge of subject
- Focused on audience needs / provides solutions
- ORIGINAL / Being human

WHAT THE BUSINESS AUDIENCE LIKE

- Personal Vs Business
- Emotion vs Logic
- Stories vs Facts
- Interactive vs Passive
- Fun vs Serious

THE UNDER PINNING RULES

- PREPARE.PREPARE. PREPARE
- Be different, be interesting every time
- Facts tell, stories charm, love sells
- Start on time, finish on time always
- PROP it up
- Let your body do the talking
- Who do you know who…

Live Sessions
Dialogue between Varun and Kabeer

K1: What is the difference between money and wealth.?

V1: Wealth is owning assets that grow over time without your further input. Wealth comes from the old English 'weal,' which means wealth, welfare, and well-being. Weal is related to the older word 'well,' meaning in a state of good fortune, welfare, or happiness. Conversely, money is merely the means of distributing wealth and time. Simply put, the equity you own in a growing "electric charger" making company is wealth; the cash you pay to buy the charger is money.

K2: Why are we called a poor or developing country? What is the difference between a developed nation and a developing nation.?

V2: Great Question. It all lies in the education, the seed. Here are some facts: India ranks 23rd in financial literacy among 28 countries, according to Visa.

Did You Know

Top 10 most Financially literate countries (%)

Denmark - 71%, Norway 71%, Sweden 71%, Canada 68%, United Kingdom 67%, Germany 66%, Netherlands 66%, Australia 64%, Finland - 63%.

For the latest data, please connect with us.

K3: Why is the financial literacy rate so low in India?

V3: Without mincing words, it is solely because of education, and with the advent of AI and regenerative AI, every passing day is getting irrelevant, outdated, and time pass. And we all know that time is money! The evil lies at the root of education, which at one point in time produced the emperors the universe has never seen. Macauley found the secret and destroyed it, and though Britishers left us physically, in our minds, Macauley has been living and enjoying for three hundred years and counting.

Did You Know

Out of the total population, only 24 % of the Indian population is financially literate. About 76 percent of Indian adults do not even understand the basics of financial management, and the worst is that 80 percent of women in India struggle with financial illiteracy. India also deals with tremendous inter-state differences. Metropolitan areas like Maharashtra, Delhi, and West Bengal have 17%, 32%, and 21% financial literacy rates, respectively. At the same time, states like Bihar, Rajasthan, Jharkhand, and Uttar Pradesh, where poverty is rampant, suffer from low literacy rates. While Goa has the highest literacy rate of 50 percent, Chhattisgarh lacks financial education and has the lowest literacy rate of 4 percent.

For the latest data, please connect with us.

K4: It feels like a grim situation. I see myself here and feel blessed to acquire such valuable knowledge, but then what is the solution? How can more youths like me in darkness get this practical knowledge and live a prosperous life?

V4: Yes, it is a dangerous situation for society. One solution is to keep blaming Macaulay and fight with the system to remove him! The Ghost of Macaulay, you know what I mean! So, the best way is to create more financially literate and entrepreneurial youths outside the ghost system! Let go, the ghost! And become the change you want to see! That is why the moment we got the idea of creating an MBA-like crash course for you, it was a eureka moment for us because this program has the potential to help millions of youths in India acquire practical business and human management knowledge and develop entrepreneurial mindset at a fraction of time and cost, without going to college again and falling in the Macauley's apple trap, the degree trap, I mean. Remember, the fact is that 55% of MBAs remain jobless. As I write, our country's top business management institution could not place 100% of students even for internships.

K5: What is the meaning of startup?

V5: Startups are young companies founded to develop a unique product or service, bring it to market, and make it irresistible and irreplaceable for customers. A startup works like any other company. I.e., a group of employees or friends working together to create a product or service that customers will buy. What distinguishes a startup from other businesses, though, is the way a startup goes about doing that. Rooted in innovation, a startup aims to remedy existing product deficiencies or create new categories of goods and services, disrupting entrenched ways of thinking and doing business for entire industries. That is why many Startups are known within their respective sectors as "disruptors".

K6: In that case there must be many different types of startups?

V6: Startups are categorized into six types:

Types Of Startups

- Scalable Startups
- Small business startups
- Lifestyle startups
- Buyable startups
- Big Business startups
- Social startups

K7: What type of startups we are?

V7: We are a small business startup. My Goal is to make a scalable startup by developing a proprietary automated portfolio management software which will have a minimum guaranteed returned based on number of years a client would like to be invested and the processes of onboarding to exit will be AI driven. Varun added, so if you were wondering why I chose you to be my second in command, now you know the secret. Kabeer, was feeling on cloud nine and blushing, Varun could see the happiness and pride on Kabeer's face and Varun was also feeling happy with the quality of questions Kabeer was asking. Remember a true master always judge a student by the quality of questions he or she asks, not by marks or degrees.

K8: Dad mentioned that 80% of startups fail within one year; why? How have you survived for five years?

V8: This is a great question, and only those trained by Gyan can ask this quality of question. So, while there could be many reasons, the research says, given a situation, 80% of all humans think and act alike, and no wonder why 80% of startups fail every year; all are like-minded, educated degree holders! The following are the significant reasons why startups fail:

Why Startups Fail

(I) Is the team passionate about the idea? It is all in execution. Even an outstanding concept can fail to engage its audience if the team is not ready to do everything to support it.

(II) Do the founders have domain expertise? The founders should know everything about the space in which they operate.

(III) Are they willing to put in the time? Early startup employees often have intense work schedules. A team must be willing to devote most of their working hours to an idea to thrive.

(IV) Why this idea, and why now? Is this a new idea? If so, why have people not tried it before? If not, what makes the startup team uniquely able to crack the code?

(V) How big is the market? The size of a startup's market defines the scale of its opportunity. Too small an opportunity market size may lead to financials that are not large enough to attract the investors' attention as they look for 5x, 10x plus returns on their investments.

Now, the other part of the question: How have I survived? Mine is a self-funded business. I have yet to open for external investors, and here lies the secret of my success. I have seen millions of young and early-age startup founders making a grave mistake by plunging into business just because they have a great product or idea. They get falsely guided by mentors or business coaches they see on social media platforms that they will bring investors and build unicorns by purchasing their self-paced course for just Rs. 100/-. Through your question, let the message reach the millions of aspiring and early-stage entrepreneurs that it is great to have a product. It is great to have an idea, but before taking a plunge into business, go through my above seven reasons why startups fail, and if you think you can still succeed, ensure to have your business model defined in such a way that for five years even if no investor comes, you will be able to run your business profitably. The calamity is that millions of early-stages and aspiring entrepreneurs I meet being part of the investor community myself, 90% of startup founders have no idea what business modelling means, and this is the root cause of 80% of startups failing within one year and only 10% surviving beyond five years.

K9: Would you teach me, business modeling? It looks difficult that is why many youths and entrepreneurs do not know? Though dad had told me the other day, anything is as difficult or easy as much I am prepared for.

V9: It is certainly not easy, making foundation is the most important and difficult of task in the process of creating a structure. Experts are needed, patience is needed, preparation is needed and that is precisely myself and Gyan decided to prepare a strong foundation for you rather than you depending on Vikram to give you lecture on business model and you land up living in a building which is built on a false structure just like degrees ! it gives you feeling that you know , but you do not know and the irony , you do not even know what you do not know ! the ultimate confusion, the outcome of degree! in fact 90% of entrepreneurs are exactly in this situation, in mess, searching for mentors, business coaches, motivational speakers, because they do not even know the reason of why their business is failing or why their career is stagnating .So, we want you to learn the art of business modeling so you know for yourself how to build the foundation of your own business on which you can design the business of your dreams and build wealth not only for ourselves but for all your customers and generations to come.

K10: Have you already spoken to investors? How does a startup raise funds?

V10: Yes. Indeed, I have. In fact, for over 20 years, I have helped global investors make a great deal of returns from their investments, and they are willing to invest with me at any stage. Still, I am holding myself because, in return, I must promise X% of returns, and I want to ensure it is the best in the industry, therefore preparing the foundation, and you are going to be one of the pillars! But for your understanding, Startups generally raise money via several rounds of funding:

How Do Startups Raise Funds

(I) A preliminary round is known as bootstrapping when the founders, friends, and family invest in the business.

(II) Afterward comes seed funding from so-called "angel investors," high net-worth individuals who invest in early-stage companies.

(III) Next, there are series A, B, C, and D funding rounds, primarily led by venture capital firms that invest hundreds of millions of dollars into companies.

(IV) Finally, a startup may decide to become a public company and open itself to outside money via IPO, an acquisition by a special purpose acquisition company (SPAC), or a direct listing on a stock exchange.

K11: Please help me understand what investors look for in a startup while making an investment decision.

V11: I am loving your questions. So, the method used is metrics, and following are investigated before being considered for investment

Key metrics investors look for in a startup before deciding to invest

- Order no's & average size of order in value terms
- Monthly Unique visitors/prospects
- Customer conversion rate
- App downloads (for app-based startup)
- Active Users/clients
- Time spent in-app (for app-based)
- Monthly Active Users (ARPU)
- GMV (Gross merchandise value)

K12: One question that is a mystery for millions of youths, even in my college, we used to discuss is how a company making million-dollar losses is called a unicorn. Investors keep investing in a loss-making company. When a small business person with a ten Lakh rupee loan from a bank goes into losses, their life becomes hell, which is why none of my friends in the college dare to think of their own business. They want to become entrepreneurs in their hearts, but somehow, they look for a job or prefer to sit at home rather than take risks for themselves and their families. Please help me in understanding.

V12: Your question is very pertinent. I would say here once again that the education that is supposed to empower youths to be what they want to be has become the education of slavery. At the same time, every institution will have a big banner at the entrance, "Empowering youths," nobody asks how! Remember, the quality of Apple matters! The only purpose of education is to develop entrepreneurs, which means empowered mindsets mean entrepreneurial mindsets. But as I said before, our education is doing sheers asana, standing upside down! So let me tell you, it takes a year to develop a youth with an entrepreneurial mindset and an empowered individual; it also encompasses the DIY activities, the techniques, the projects, the real-world learning, and much more. The reasons why educational institutions cannot develop entrepreneurial skills are numerous, ranging from syllabus to resources to time, policies, economic cycle, and many more. That is why, precisely as I said before, the roots of evil have gone too deep, and the best way is to be the change you want to see and become a part of the solution rather than fight with the ghost; that is what the mind wants, more the better, busy always, solving problems. Let go, the ghost! Drop the apple!

Now, the other part of the question is about startups making losses and still becoming unicorns; for this, we must go a little deeper and make you understand some of the concepts such as cash burn, cash flows, valuation techniques, and profit and loss concepts, which you will learn as we move further. When you have learned the necessary concepts, you will realize the best thing that can happen in the life of a man or a woman is to be an entrepreneur. Remember again, being an entrepreneur does not only mean having your business; it also means you get the power to choose, to decide, to do what you want to do, the dependent yet independent. In control, yet accessible, and that is why there is so much urge within us to build something of our own, because you face, you fail, you succeed, you live! You make others live, an act of God! So, hereafter, when you meet your friends, inform them that not all is lost and that there is an opportunity for them like you to develop an entrepreneurial mindset at a fraction of the time and cost so they can also become emperors. Now every youth of India can become an enterprenuer, an emperor.

Education is the means to empower individuals and elevate society.

Sw. Viveka Nanda

Live session Advance Level
Dialogue Between Gyan & Kabeer

K1: Dad, I have understood the product, I have understood the benefits it provides, I have understood the business model, I have understood my competition, I have understood my target market, but still, I am not confident to sell. Please help me; Uncle has given me the list of prospects and expects me to start selling next week. Why am I losing confidence?

G1: Gyan understood Kabeer is going through a situation that millions of startup founders starting fresh go through just before the product launch or making a pitch to an investor or the sales professional making their first call to a client. It is called the "cold feet" syndrome, precisely what Arjuna developed just before he was to "go for the kill." That situation led to a question-and-answer session that gave birth to the most loved, read, and practiced scripture in the universe, the "Bhagwat Geetha" The scripture which since eternity is providing and will continue to provide the light of wisdom to billions into darkness, in chaos, lord Krishna becomes the guide, the mentor, the coach, the friend to lead from non-action to action, from hopelessness to hope, makes a common man, arjuna, the legendary! So let us see how Gyan makes Kabeer move and "go for the kill"!

Knowing the delicate situation of Kabeer, Gyan had to do something miraculous to make him move, so out of the blue, he asked a question that only a 21st-century crazy father can ask his son: do you know the sex? For a moment, Kabeer felt he was going to faint! Kabeer balanced himself and said, yes, Kabeer had no choice either, I know, but what is this question, Dad! Kabeer sounded a bit irritated, but without getting bothered even a bit, Gyan continued, tell me what sex is! Kabeer looked at his father's face as if he was seeing him for the first time! Kabeer, tell me quick, the voice came from Gyan; what are you asking Dad? Stop it! Kabeer was just so embarrassed. What to stop, your job! Gyan fired back. Kabeer just realized what he had said, so he politely said, Dad, is it necessary to answer? Is there no other way to tell what you want to say? Gyan was waiting for it and replied you only said simplify! What can be more?

More straightforward than this question, we all have it! Do not waste time, Kabeer; answer me: what is sex? Why are you getting embarrassed? I have not asked with whom, how, or when; that would complicate you. For the first time, Kabeer saw his father as a flamboyant man willing to go to any length to win! So, he felt better replying than arguing for his good. He said to me sex is an experience," Gyan just jumped and said, I was expecting this from an intelligent youth like you! So now, having known what sex is, I will use the most straightforward terms with which you will be able to start selling from this moment on! Kabeer began to feel excited and said wow, this sounds great, Dad!

Gyan was serious; he knew the task at hand, so without wasting a moment, he continued, the first thing, while you have known your product and its benefits, you must make it "special," Just like everyone has sex but some make it unique in their tiny little ways like taking a holiday and spend time together, help the partner finish their work faster, switch on the room freshener with their unique fragrance, a tiny little gift to make the moment memorable, just a rose flower works! What one gives is not necessary; how one presents to make others feel special is essential, and remember, the ones who find ways to make sex special will always have more fun, more satisfaction, more happiness, more love, a long-lasting relationship, and above all desire for more! So, another name for special is more! So, find ways to make your product special, which does not mean you have to ask Varun to design another offering; this one mistake is destroying promising startups, disappearing from business within no time, and finishing the career of young and dynamic sales professionals in a way, they would never dare to sale again! What is so grave here? Never ask your company to change or modify their product because the competitor has it and is probably better than yours. Remember you must make it special if your employer has not told you the "how," and if your employer is a technical person, you forget it! Either you DIY (Do It Yourself) or look for someone else! So, once you learn the art of making your product or service "special," you have the secret key to engaging more! Remember again, just like in sex, the more time you spend with your partner in foreplay, the better the experience, the deeper the bonding and outcome, an incredible experience, a tremendous flourishing relationship. So, the first secret to success in sales is when your prospect is spending more time with you than with your competitor because you have something special! And here you have the first secret key to win a customer; hold it tight! While the other secrets follow.

The second is "extra." Being special is fine, but adding flavors is excellent! Remember this: The GIG economy has moved beyond what is special to what is extra. In most funded startups, their major part of fund gets burnt in offering that "extra flavor" for free to win the customer and kill the competition, which is technically called the customer acquisition cost and comes under the concept of "cash burn" which Varun has already taught you. So now you will be able to relate why, having million-dollar losses, startups still get more valuation and more money to burn; it is to acquire a customer at any cost, the cost which the competition cannot afford, tiny and medium business owners running businesses with their own hard-earned money or borrowed from bank on which they pay interest, and with the time they either shut or sell themselves to the startup and exit so the company gets a free runway to play the price game with the customers. There is much to understand; we will go more profound as we move together. Know this is the standard strategy of building a unicorn startup, and to me, this strategy is just like sex, which is pay and use! How! The invested money is used to offer extra for free, so as long as fund flows in, it is possible to provide extra. Hence, money is the key here, not the flavor. Here, you must note only those funded startups succeed, who, with the borrowed money, create the special effect and top it up with extra flavor rather than burning cash, and only 1% of all funded startups can achieve and win in style. So, it is perfectly suitable; 90% of funded startups fail within two years; how long can one use the money to pay for extra flavor? So, remember, your success lies in creating that "extra" value, which makes the customer feel special and enjoy the same flavor as your competitor. And let me tell you, you can outpace the competition if you can customize the flavors because you have spent more time together! And make it "extraordinary" an act of God! Remember, you will find customers always willing to pay for what has made them feel extraordinary"! Who does not want to feel extraordinary? It is an exotic feeling. Exotic and cheap! That is so middle class! And here you got the second secret key. Add it, hold; it takes two to tango!

Third, "the X factor." You probably know what it means, but you will need more words if I ask you to define it. So let me help you; imagine you reached out to your partner, you made her feel special, both of you spent a good time together at exotic locations, you both liked each other, and, one fine evening, after having dinner at a classic restaurant of her choice, you are about to drop her home, you thought this is the moment, and you proposed for "sex" and to the shock of your life, your partner asks "why you"! You would faint, or if you are strong, you would take a breath and start blabbering to convince, explain, justify, and there you miss, she has run away! Why! Because you do not have the X factor! And I know you will say, Dad, tell me quickly how to get the X factor! I desperately need her, and the more you become desperate, the more she runs away, never returning. That is why look around you; you will see desperate salesmen and women!

So, in simple words, the "X" factor is nothing but how you charm your partner, so the "why" disappears, and you become the charming magnet! Remember, the desperate salesperson "pushes," the successful salesperson "pulls," and that is just 1% of professionals, the God of sales! So here, you got the third secret key; hold it tight!

You might have already started feeling difficulty managing three keys: safekeeping, protection, and weight, so before you ask me for "a kiss," remember this as an awesome threesome secret and make it "sex," and the golden gate has opened for you to become the God of sales! The eternal winner, born to win in style.

Kabeer was in awe of his father today; he was mesmerized and charmed by how his father made him feel today; he had moved! He hugged and kissed his father! And, in a witty tone, said, let us spend some more time; let us have coffee before we do it again! Gyan smiled and saw the glow on Kabeer's face; he closed his eyes for a moment in gratitude for his master; he had won! Kabeer just kissed

Live session Advance Level

Dialogue between Varun and Kabeer

K1: What is transformation? What is digital transformation? Is it needed?

V1: This is paradoxical.! To be or not to be. To do or not to do. Out of the two choices, it is better to do. But why! Human Nature is to enquire to know more and do more! So, any transformation results from the human being having a "thinking mind." That means humans cannot remain idle or be as they are. Therefore, remember that "desire" is the secret behind all transformations, you and I included!

The first part, transformation, is a process in which the old disappears completely. The outcome is also called revolution. For example, think of a wheel made from wooden pieces. The making of the wheel not only changed the original shape of the wood, the origin of which is a tree, but it also changed the way humanity lived, the revolution which became the foundation for millions of inventions, the "speed"! Remember, we might feel transformation, revolution, and innovation are one, but they are not.

Now, who invented the wheel, where, when, and how? That is fine; it is an ordinary question. What about thinking of how the thought of a wheel in the first place came? You may find it crazy, but remember, quality matters, so let us ask where the idea came from! Was Newton sitting under the tree waiting with the thought of an apple falling, or did an apple fell and, at that moment, a quality question transformed an ordinary man into a legendary scientist? Was Buddha sitting under the tree waiting for enlightenment? It is, in fact, otherwise; he was tired of seeking, searching, and asking! That night, he decided to drop all thinking and doing, and magic happened in that moment: an ordinary man became the most intelligent and scientific God humanity has seen.

What I am trying to tell you here is, think, and you will find all the transformational inventions are existential; the man just became the medium, the accidental. So, remember what you see outside as transformational or revolutionary, be it a human or an object;

remember the origin; the root is inside, in existence. Here I am sharing a secret of a lifetime; if you look around for the past hundred years, there have been fewer transformational inventions; instead, you will see more transformational destructions, also called weapons of mass destruction, atom bombs, nuclear bombs, biological bombs, missiles, etc. What is happening? Simple, education inside, transformation outside. So, I am sure you will now need no other example to understand that a better tomorrow is a hopeless hope. And by no means do I intend to say live hopeless! My whole effort is to make you full of life. So, what is the way out? The way is inside out! This process is called transformation, and it is the simplest: just being more with your heart, being more with trees, being more with the sun, being more with the moon, the stars, the rivers, with yourself, the moment comes! The moment is already there; you are not in the moment. Here, it would help if you remembered that our entire education was existential, inside out in our country's golden era and civilization. I hope it is clear to you that if you want to become a legendary professional and a human being, you need to spend time with your heart; existence is waiting to whisper; it is whispering, listen and transform, become one in billions, the legendary, here, and now.

K2: Why has Digital transformation become the Key for businesses to survive and grow?

V2: The education of mind, which is always running, needs more money, business, and success. Therefore, we must explore the world market for new business opportunities, demand creation, and generation, and it has to be super-fast because everyone is running for the kingdom! So we are in a universal race, and to keep up with the fundamentals of earning more, we must follow the philosophy of producing cheaper, i.e., lesser cost, higher quality, for which we need to have quality systems in place to enhance consumer experience! The secret Key to building a business that lasts for centuries. So, it is now a whole of technology's work to predict human taste and instincts, which earlier was limited to identifying, analysing, and fulfilling. Now, AI, Artificial Intelligence, is all about: igniting the sleeping desire! Desire and run! Men have become useless. So, it is better to say behind every legendary business, there is a machine!

K3: Is Digital Transformation Good or Bad?

V3: We have no choice. It is now an irreversible process. We live in the 21st century, in a GIG economy, a connected and complicated world; 99% of us can earn, survive, and live because of technology. If we take technology away from our lives, what will be left? Only one question: who am I? Here, we must also remember all transformations or revolutions, whether digital, industrial, or astronomical, are of no use if it has not added to the development of human consciousness, which means the growth of human qualities, which means the quality of heart, which is love, compassion, and empathy, and here let me be straight, it is obvious the kind of technological advancement the world has made, the earth would have been heaven to live, that better tomorrow would have come centuries ago. But it is a calamity that with every technological advancement, more men, more women, more children, more animals, more trees, more mountains, more rivers are killed and destroyed, and who knows, with a child, a newton is killed, with a man, a buddha is killed. It looks like, this time, Life has been waiting for centuries to dance and celebrate. You are the only hope of Life.

"Respect life, revere life.
There is nothing more holy than life,
nothing more divine than life."

OSHO

GLIMPSES OF BUSINESS MANAGEMENT WORKSHOP

IT TAKES WHAT IT TAKES TO BE
THE LEGENDARY WEALTH CREATORS

5 YEAR RETUNS (%)

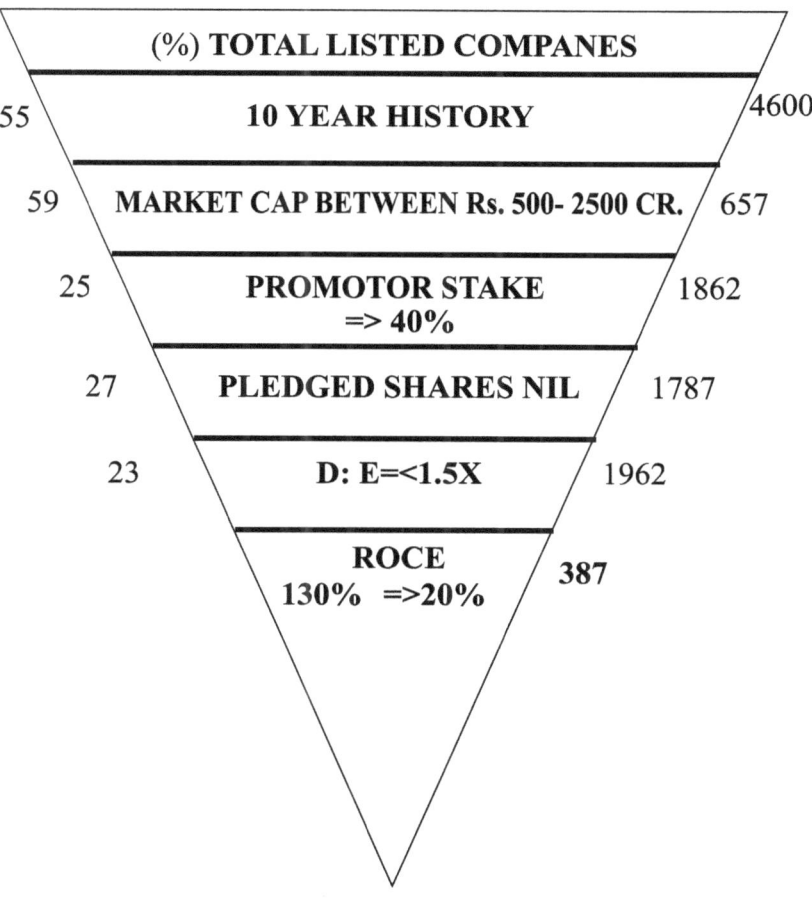

- Data presented are of previous financial years.
  For latest data, please write to us at info@pkconsulting.in

BUSINESS MODELING

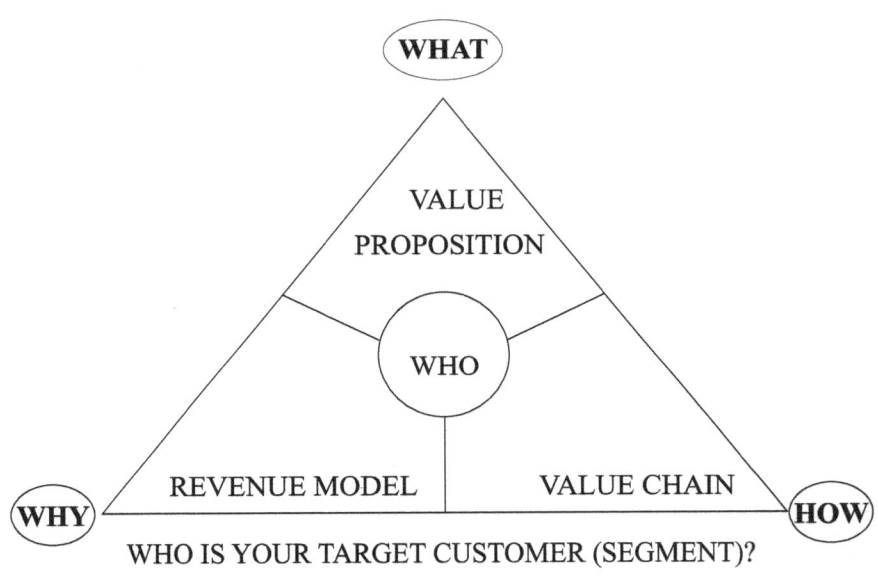

WHAT - What do you do! What do you offer to the customer!

HOW - How do you do! How is the value proposition created!

WHY - Why do you do, what you do! Which problem you are solving for a Better tomorrow!

INNER MODELING

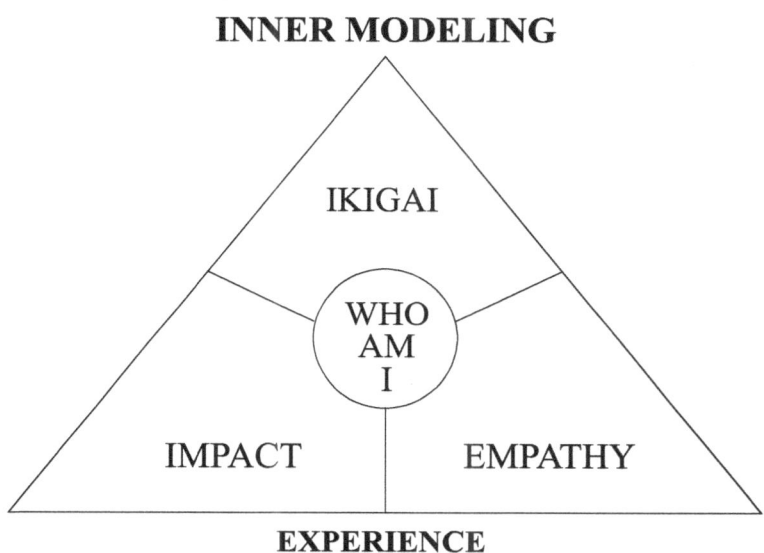

IKIGAI-	Life's purpose. Meaning of life. Talent, passion, profession
IMPACT-	The one in billions. The legendary. Living in the hearts
EMPATHY-	We are love. Love knows no other. All in one, one in all
EXPERIENCE-	Life is an experience. Make it yours. Write your own story

The 21ˢᵗ century successful entrepreneurial mindsets

Inner Modeling

Business Modeling

KEY COMPONENTS OF A SUCCESSFUL BUSINESS MODEL

- What does the company manufacture
- What is its capacity to produce that product/s
- What is the brand image
- Entry barrier for the business
- Who are the competitors
- Competitive position of the company vis a vis the others in the same industry.
- How are the profit margins, how much is the market share.

WHY SOME BUSINESSES WILL ALWAYS DO WELL FEATURES OF A GOOD BUSINESS

- Clean accounting
- NIL or Low NC and related party transactions
- Present in essential category
- Monopoly or dominant market share
- Very Low or zero Debt.
- Cost effective and size advantage
- Huge runaway for future growth
- Consistent earnings growth power
- Strong free and operating cash flows
- Strong capital allocation by management
- Visionary management
- High switching cost (customer capturing)

KEY QUALITIES OF SUCCESSFUL ENTREPRENUERS

- Invests in a business not in stock market.
- Knows Low or Zero Debt. is a way of business and of life.
- Knows Low Cash conversion cycle is one of the keys of good business model.
- Keeps track of sectoral trends as a good investing habit.
- Knows Capital management / utilization is the key of a successful business.

WHY STOCK MARKETS ARE IMPORTANT FOR US

Myths Vs. Reality

- Stock markets forms the primary source of capital for existing and new business owners to raise capital in efficient manner.
- Stock market allows retail investors to get an ownership of businesses via IPO or public issue.
- Equity as an asset class cannot be ignored.
- Stock markets are called wheels or barometer of the economy.
- Have generated far more better returns compare to any other asset class. about 15% over 20 years.
- Capital raised helps companies expand operations create more jobs.
- Active mutual fund investing in equity markets have made it a preferred asset class with easy liquidity option.

CHECK LIST FOR FILTERING COMPANIES - LONG TERM INVESTING
Manufacturing Companies

- ROCE => 15%
- OCF/EBITDA =>50%
- D: E =< 1.5
- PROMOTOR STAKE >40%
- PRMOTOR PEDGE = 0
- ROE => 15% (must not be used for cyclical or commodity sectors)
- ROIC => 15%
- OCF/EBITDA =>50%
- CASH CONVERSION CYCLE = 60 DAYS
- DUPONT ANALYSIS = ROE = NET MARGIN * ASSET TURNOVER *Flv.
- TAX @25%.
- NC and NC related transactions
- Goodwill - Large is not good.
- Related party transactions as % to sales, net worth and net profits.
- Depreciation & Capex.
- Cash tax to PBT. < 25% not good.

THE SECRET CODE OF WEALTH CREATION

GROW YOUR WEALTH BY
@ 15% YEAR ON YEAR

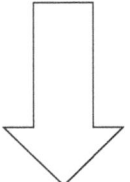

NOMINAL GDP = GDP + INFLATION

- RECOMMENDED AGE -20 YEARS ONWARDS

BEST INTRDAY TRADERS BEST PRACTISES
Recommended for beginners and early stage traders

- Always comes well prepared in the morning with complete after-market studies. Starts the day at eight thirty mornings sharp.
- Always wait and observes the setup before punching the trade.
- Always trades on stocks with high volume in the first hour, i.e., 9.15 am - 10.15 am.
- Always look for candle structure as advised during the training.
- Keep the risk-reward ratio at 1:1 for the first six months and increase it gradually to 2 in steps of 0.25.
- Always follows disciplined trading timings, i.e., 9 am 10.30 am, morning and 1.00 pm 2.30 pm, afternoon.

- In the beginning, focuses on identifying structures and observations rather than looking at P&L and taking trades.
- Starts with Rs. 25,000/- in account. Keeps stop loss at Rs. 250/- maximum for first hundred trades. Deviating from this rule will ensure you will get out of the stock market, never to come back, i.e., losing the opportunity to become a youth millionaire.
- Mentally preparesto hit stop loss in the first 100 trades.

INTRADAY TRADING EXECUTION CHEAT SHEET

- Wait for the first 5 minutes of the candle to complete. Check where the stock has opened compared to yesterday's levels.
- Mark the buy & sell zone within 15 minutes. Otherwise, do not trade. Check the volume. Leave that stock if the volume has not reached its highest in at least the last five days.
- Check 20,200 DMA levels.
- Look for a sideways zone always. After 15 minutes, look carefully at least three candles before punching the trade.
- Mark the support and resistance levels.
- To begin with, trade Nifty 50 stocks only.
- Only take a trade if yesterday's Low or yesterday's high is breached.

Every Beginning Has An End

Friends, this brings me to the end of the live sessions. I hope you will find my book "Sexful" and will experiment with the techniques to become the extraordinary millennial of the 21st century. I would love to hear about your experiences. You can write or connect with me; my coordinates are at the end of the book.

I also know many of you would want to see the outcome of my story; what happened to Kabeer after the completion of the "Real World Bootcamp"? Did Kabeer become the godly salesman and the legendary investment banker? Did Varun achieve his goal of making V&V a unicorn with Kabeer by his side?

It would have been easy for me to paint a successful outcome like the Hindi movies; in the end, all is well, and the hero wins! Before responding to your questions, I want to give a little work to your mind, and I ask you! who do you think is the hero in the story, Kabeer, Gyan, Varun, or someone else? And your reason for thinking so. I would love to hear your thoughts.

Now, to answer your question: Kabeer has become one of the world's best salesman and transformational human being. Anything less, he would have failed his masters, Gyan and Varun. But the transformation journey was arduous, and there were moments when he felt he was developing cold feet! And in those moments, he will kiss his father, Gyan, in thoughts! And move on to win in style.

I promise to share Kabeer's journey of becoming a legendary investment banker if you ask me sincerely! Thinking how? You know the secret!

DO-IT-YOURSELF TECHNIQUES

DIY

Activity Preface

While I would love to share all the activities that Gyan and Varun asked Kabeer to do, it will become an Ekalavya and Dronacharya story, but I want you to hold the secret tight with your thumb on! So, try practicing a few. Whether you are an early-stage or aspiring entrepreneur or a graduate, if you have read the "sex technique," sincerely, the DIY activities will make you think differently! Know that you have changed the quality. You have dropped the apple! You have found your way to the Garden of Eden, to the kingdom of God.! Remember the famous quote, "Think outside the BOX"! Do it here and now.

INNER MODELING
Self Counselling

- Who you think you are?
- What you want to become?
- Are you happy now?
- What is your one ultimate desire?
- Three subjects you liked during your studies or would like to know or study in future.
- Why do you think you like these subjects what application of these subjects, you see in real world, personal or professional?
- What do you think the current education is lacking for you to make a career choice, personally and professionally?
- What is that one desire which you feel strongly about if filled will make you happy?
- What makes you happy now?
- Given a choice which field you would like to take up the job or build your own startup?

- If you have been given INR one lakh today, what would you do with it?
- What love means to you?
- Who is that one person you love the most and why? what comes to your mind when you think or hear the word money?
- What do you think according to you could be the purpose of doing a job or business?
- Do you think that you have been sufficiently informed or taught about money while in school or college?
- Do you feel the necessity of knowing everything about money while you are in school or college. or you think it is not an area for you to know?
- Please tell me one person that you dream of meeting now, one company that you want to work for now or in the future? one place that you want to visit, one thing that you want to do other than your job or business.
- Which skills, you think you need to learn to have to get a good job or do your own startup which has not been taught to you in college?

Please Note

If you work with the above questions and answers, you must be able to find your Ikigai. You will become the master of your destiny. Alone, you will be enough. In the process, if you develop "cold feet" with any questions, remember me! My coordinates are mentioned at the end of the book. Please write or connect with me; I will gladly help you move!

BUSINESS MODELING

PLEASE ANSWER THE FOLLOWING

- Why are you into the business?
- Why are you into this line (product/service) of business?
- What problem your product or service is solving for your customer?
- Why the customer is buying from you?
- One problem you wish if solves right now you can grow your sales by how many times in how many months?
- Who is your closest competitor? Why do you consider them as competitor?

Please Note

If you are an entrepreneur and can work with the above questions and answers, I guarantee you will not need any mentor or a business coach in life. If you pitch your business to investors, the chances of getting the funding will increase; remember quality matters. If you develop "cold feet" with any of the questions, remember me! My coordinates are at the end of the book. Please write or connect with me; together, we can move mountains!

Project Work-1 (Group/individual)

- Create source of funds.
- Create an inventory (product or service).
- Make the quarterly cash flow statement (one quarter).
- Present the profit and loss report to the board.
- List the top 10 companies in the wealth management sector by market cap and brand value and present to the board your plan of action to put the company into the league of the top ten.

Project Work -2 (Group/Individual)

- What is your company's monthly budget on maintaining digital infrastructure?
- Which digital tools you or your company use in day-to-day operations?
- Name two challenges in implementing and managing digital tools.
- Name three digital initiatives that you have implemented to reduce manual labor and enhance customer experience.
- Make the marketing budget for a quarter and present the ROI to the board.

> **Please note**
>
> Consider the above project activity as a three-month on-the-job internship of Kabeer. You might think, how can you answer these questions without being on the job? That is a great sign; you have started thinking differently! So, try doing the projects with your fellow friends or colleagues, or you can also engage your parents or siblings or ask your teachers if they could help you create a group amongst your classmates and make the projects one of the assignments. I would love to hear about your experience in the project, the challenges you faced, and how you overcame them. If you develop "cold feet" in the process, remember me! My coordinates are mentioned at the end of the book. Do write or connect with me. Together, we will make it Kiss.

THE CLOSING PRAYERS

O God! I have not seen you; I do not know where you live, I do not know whether you are a man or a woman, but I know you are my breath, you are my heartbeat, I exist in your nature, I live under your sky, I eat your food, I walk on your land, you gave me my loving mother and father, you gave me mind to think, but I considered it all mine. Pl. forgive me for the sin; I have forgotten who I am, I am lost, I am trying but unable to find my way home, I have become weak, I am fearful, I am alone. O God, you have sent me to the world; you are my Godfather; hold me, protect me, guide me, take me home; I am praying to you, God.

Home is where the heart is.

Pray. Hold. Walk. Reach

About Girish kashwani

Girish began his professional journey as an IT consultant in 1998 after graduating as an electronics engineer from Bangalore.

For over 20 years, now as a business growth advisor, Girish has been instrumental in writing success stories of hundreds of entrepreneurs and professionals, helping them grow their businesses and attain leadership positions.

Girish believes the 21st century will be the century of GIG professionals with entrepreneurial mindsets, and the current education system is unfit to develop youths as global professionals and human beings, the fundamental qualities of an entrepreneurial mind.

Girish believes the only education needed to develop youths as extraordinary millennials is the education of developing entrepreneurial mindsets, a mind made of heart.

Through this book, Girish intends to reach out to millions of youths and professionals worldwide to develop them as global professionals and human beings at a fraction of the time and cost compared to a regular degree program, irrespective of their academic performance and current stage of career be it Job or early stage of building their startup.

Author's Coordinates

Postal address

Pk Consulting
Golden Square, #1101, 24th main, JP Nagar, 1st phase
(above ICICI bank), Bangalore 560078
Phone: - (91) 080-42711000
Website : www.pkconsulting.in

E-mail

To share your **experiences** about the book - gk@pkconsulting.in
For **enrollment** in the real world bootcamp - info@pkconsulting.in

Connect at socials

@facebook

@Linkedin

@insta

Notes

Notes

www.ingramcontent.com/pod-product-compliance
Lightning Source LLC
LaVergne TN
LVHW041946070526
838199LV00051BA/2926